Religion in the Public Square

Point / Counterpoint
Philosophers Debate Contemporary Issues
General Editors: James P. Sterba and Rosemarie Tong

This new series provides a philosophical angle to debates currently raging in academic and larger circles. Each book is a short volume (around 200 pages) in which two prominent philosophers debate different sides of an issue. Future topics might include the canon, the ethics of abortion rights, and the death penalty. For more information contact Professor Sterba, Department of Philosophy, University of Notre Dame, Notre Dame IN 46566, or Professor Tong, Department of Philosophy, Davidson College, Davidson, NC 28036.

Political Correctness: For and Against
  Marilyn Friedman, Washington University, St. Louis
  Jan Narveson, University of Waterloo, Ontario, Canada

Humanitarian Intervention: Just War vs. Pacifism
  Robert L. Phillips, University of Connecticut
  Duane L. Cady, Hamline University

Affirmative Action: Social Justice or Unfair Preference?
  Albert G. Mosley, Ohio University
  Nicholas Capaldi, University of Tulsa

Religion in the Public Square: The Place of Religious Convictions in Political Debate
  Robert Audi, University of Nebraska
  Nicholas Wolterstorff, Yale University

Sexual Harassment: A Debate
  Linda LeMoncheck
  Mane Hajdin, University of Waikato

Religion in the Public Square

The Place of Religious Convictions in Political Debate

Robert Audi
and
Nicholas Wolterstorff

ROWMAN & LITTLEFIELD PUBLISHERS, INC.
Lanham • Boulder • New York • London

ROWMAN & LITTLEFIELD PUBLISHERS, INC.

Published in the United States of America
by Rowman & Littlefield Publishers, Inc.
4720 Boston Way, Lanham, Maryland 20706

3 Henrietta Street
London WC2E 8LU, England

British Cataloging in Publication Information Available

Library of Congress Cataloging-in-Publication Data
Audi, Robert, 1941–
    Religion in the public square : the place of religious convictions
  in political debate / Robert Audi and Nicholas Wolterstorff.
      p.   cm. — (Point / counterpoint)
    Includes bibliographical references and index.
    ISBN 0-8476-8341-9 (cloth : alk. paper). — ISBN 0-8476-8342-7
    (pbk. : alk. paper)
      1. Democracy—Religious aspects.   2. Democracy—Religious aspects—
  Christianity.   3. Religion and politics.   4. Religion and state.
  5. Religion and politics—United States.   6. Religion and state—
  United States.   7. United States—Religion.   8. United States—
  Politics and government.   I. Wolterstorff, Nicholas.   II. Title.
  III. Series.
  BL65.P7A83   1997
  291.1'77—dc20   96-44646
                                                              CIP

ISBN 0-8476-8341-9 (cloth : alk. paper)
ISBN 0-8476-8342-7 (pbk. : alk. paper)

Printed in the United States of America

CONTENTS

PREFACE

The relation between religion and politics is a perennial concern of political philosophy, but it has never been more important than it is now. Separation of church and state is being widely challenged and vigorously debated. There is a growing conviction that religious ideals should play a larger role in leading modern societies through the crises of our age, and there is—sometimes among the same people—a widespread fear that the religious zeal of some may abridge the freedom of others. Special interest groups motivated by religious concerns are lobbying for political action; fundamentalist religious movements in many parts of the world are exercising enormous influence in many nations and controlling some of them. In the United States and other liberal democracies, the legal community is reassessing the historical commitment to church-state separation.

This book has two main aims. First, we present reasoned statements of the two most important contemporary views of religion and politics—the liberal position that calls for their separation and the theologically oriented position that takes religious considerations to be not only appropriate in political debates and decisions but indispensable to the vitality of pluralistic democracy. Second, each of us offers a critique of the other's position. The debate is conducted with a focus both on principles of conduct and on concrete examples that illustrate and test them: abortion, public school prayer, religiously inspired welfare programs, vouchers to assist parents in sending their children to private schools, religious exemptions from the draft, and other current issues.

Essay 1, by Robert Audi, represents the liberal view and argues that government should be *neutral* toward religion and that religion and politics should be—in a certain way—separate both at the level of church and state and in the political conduct of individuals. Essay 2, by Nicholas Wolterstorff, represents the theologically oriented position and argues that government need only be *impartial* toward the plurality of religions and that religion and politics should not be separated either at the church-state level or in political interactions among individuals. The final essay (pp. 167–74) highlights points of agreement and difference between the authors and formulates some remaining problems for both political theorists and conscientious citizens regardless of their religious orientation.

We have sought to present our ideas and proposals with sufficient clarity and concreteness to make the book intelligible to undergraduates and with sufficient rigor and documentation to make it a resource for professional writers in the field. The book explores topics ranging from civic virtue and ethical obligation to constitutional interpretation and the foundations of democracy; from secular evidence and justification to theological commitment and faith; and from freedom of expression to the ethical limits on political action.

Each of us has benefitted from responses by far more people than we have been able to acknowledge in our essays. We are quite aware that we have not solved—or even addressed—all of the problems brought to our attention. We hope, however, that the volume will be valuable for a wide range of readers in ethics, law, political science, religion, social-political philosophy, and other fields. We also hope that it may contribute both to theory and practice: to understanding the foundations of liberal democracy and to the capacity for citizenship therein.

LIBERAL DEMOCRACY AND THE PLACE OF RELIGION IN POLITICS

Robert Audi

The relation between religion and democracy is among the most important topics in political philosophy, and the present age has brought the subject into worldwide prominence. Religious fundamentalism is a powerful force in many parts of the world, and, in some of its forms, it is hostile to democracy. There is much division of judgment regarding how much (if at all) fundamentalism may be undermining democracy in the United States, but there is little disagreement on the growing influence of the "religious right," as it is often called, in American political life. The reference is usually to conservative Christian elements, whether fundamentalist or not, but similar concerns have been expressed about fundamentalist elements in other religions and in other cultures. It must not be thought, however, that liberal religious groups are not also politically active, nor should it be assumed that religiously conservative people as such are less than strongly committed to preserving democratic government. I shall indeed assume that in the United States, at least, reflective religious people, particularly those in what we might loosely call the Hebraic-Christian tradition, are on the whole committed to preserving not only democratic government but also religious liberty, including the liberty to remain outside any religious tradition.

Both democratic government and religious liberty are values that, from the point of view of political philosophy, seem eminently worth preserving. Their joint preservation, however, is far from easy, particularly when politically active religious groups are passionately convinced that certain freedoms are religiously forbidden or are immoral or both, as in the case of abortion and physician-assisted suicide. It is in part to achieve that joint preservation that liberal democracies characteristically observe a separation of religious institutions—churches for short—and the state. It is also partly in the interest of this joint preservation that conscientious citizens in such societies seek a related separation between religious and political considerations. Both kinds of separation are major concerns in this essay.

The first aspect of church-state separation that we should note is the prohibition of governmental establishment of a religion. This prohibition is famously expressed in the First Amendment of the United States Constitution but is not built into every democratic system of government, as the histories of Western Europe and Scandinavia amply illustrate. A liberal democracy, conceived as a free and democratic society, must protect religious liberty; this is at least a strong prima facie reason for its avoiding the establishment or promotion of any particular religion.[1] The protection of religious liberty and the avoidance of a state-established religion are widely considered to be among the liberal democratic elements that justify some kind of separation of church and state. But what kind, and how much? And if there should be a measure of separation between religious institutions and the state, should there be, in our conduct as citizens, a related separation between religious and secular considerations? The question is not a sociological one concerning whether religion and politics can be mixed; they *are* mixed and will continue to be mixed. Politicians will persist in invoking the support of God; churches will continue to take political positions; and religious citizens will continue to support legislation they see as religiously desirable. But there is much to be said about what might constitute a good mixture of the religious and the political and about how to achieve a democratic harmony in producing it.

There are broadly moral arguments that support liberal democracy—the liberal democratic state—as a form of government. If any of these succeeds, then insofar as separation of church and state is crucial for liberal democracy, there is moral support for preserving that separation. Among the moral arguments one might appeal to are the following, which I state only in outline. A liberal democratic state might be held to be the only kind that preserves freedom and provides adequate scope for individual autonomy. It may also be thought to be the only kind that can sustain legitimate government, which may be broadly construed as the sort of government that rational citizens are willing to consent to. It may be held to contribute best—or to be essential—to human flourishing. And there are other rationales for preferring liberal democracy over alternative forms of government. I assume here that some such rationale, when fully developed, will succeed. But it also seems to me that religious institutions might, for internal reasons, want to subsist in a liberal state. They might, for one thing, religiously endorse a moral case for a liberal state. But they might also see such a state as best for their own flourishing, especially in a world of inescapable religious pluralism.

Individual citizens, religious and non-religious alike, often have a similar considered desire to live in a free and democratic society in which religious liberty is assiduously preserved. I assume that this desire is reasonable, nor will I argue for the preferability of liberal democracy over other forms of government. My task here is to explore some appropriate liberal democratic principles in all three areas of conduct: that of the state, that of religious institutions, and that of individual citizens.

Separation of Church and State as Addressed to the State

Historically, the idea that there should be a separation between church and state concerns chiefly those two entities conceived institutionally: as large-scale social units rather than merely as collections of loosely affiliated people acting as individuals. Some of the issues raised by institutional separation have counterparts in the lives of individuals and will be discussed below. My first concern, however, is the large-scale separation viewed mainly as constraining governments in relation to the religious institutions under their jurisdiction.

If we think of the theory of separation of church and state as applied to governmental institutions in relation to religious ones, we find at least three basic principles in any full-blooded liberal version of the separation view.[2] These are bound together by the ideal of religious liberty as a central element in a free society. But other ideals, such as those of the equal basic rights of persons regardless of their religious affiliation, of unfettered democratic participation, of social pluralism, and, more generally, of human flourishing, can also unify and support the various elements in the institutional theory of separation of church and state.

The first principle—which I shall call *the libertarian principle*— says that the state must permit the practice of any religion, though within certain limits.[3] This is a principle of tolerance. The second principle—*the equalitarian principle*—says that the state may not give preference to one religion over another. This is a principle of impartiality. The principle not only rules out an established church— whose existence might be plausibly argued to be consistent with the libertarian principle—but also precludes such practices as legally requiring a certain religious affiliation as a condition for public office. The third principle—*the neutrality principle*—is less commonly affirmed, but also belongs to any full-blooded liberal account of separation of church and state. It says that the state should neither favor nor disfavor religion (or the religious) *as such*, that is, give positive or negative preference to institutions or persons simply because they are religious. As its name indicates, this is a principle of neutrality, not only neutrality among religions but between the religious and the non-religious.

Why should a free and democratic society endorse these three principles? This is a large question, and I shall cite only the most general supporting grounds. I take the principles in turn.

The libertarian principle

It seems to me beyond dispute that from the moral point of view a society without religious liberty is simply not adequately free. Moreover, freedom is required for democracy, at least in any sense of 'democracy' relevant here. Thus, if one's ideal is a free and democratic society, one wants a social (presumably constitutional) framework to guarantee at least this much religious liberty: (1) freedom of religious belief, understood to prohibit the state or anyone else from forcibly inculcating religious beliefs in the general population[4]; (2) freedom of worship, involving, minimally, a right of peaceable religious assembly, as well as a right to offer prayers by oneself; and

(3) freedom to engage in (and to teach one's children if one has any) the rites and rituals of one's religion, provided these practices do not violate certain basic moral rights. Clearly, then, a free and democratic society should adopt the libertarian principle. A society without the freedom that it guarantees would offer inadequate protection against governmental coercion.

I cannot here try to define 'religious,' but it must for our purposes be taken sufficiently narrowly to permit a distinction between the moral and the religious, so that, e.g., not just any seriously held moral belief counts as religious. The issues that most concern us are those in which some theistic religion figures. Non-theistic religions pose—other things equal—far less serious church-state problems.

It may help in understanding what constitutes a religion to keep in mind nine important features, each of which is relevant, though not strictly necessary, to a social institution's constituting a religion: (1) belief in supernatural beings; (2) a distinction between sacred and profane objects; (3) ritual acts focused on those objects; (4) a moral code believed to be sanctioned by the god(s); (5) religious feelings (awe, mystery, etc.) that tend to be aroused by the sacred objects and during rituals; (6) prayer and other communicative forms concerning the god(s); (7) a world view according the individual a significant place in the universe; (8) a more or less comprehensive organization of one's life based on the world view; and (9) a social organization bound together by the preceding.[5] The richest paradigms of religion, such as Christianity, Judaism, and Islam, exhibit all of these features and in virtue of that are especially good cases to consider in determining what constitutes an appropriate separation of church and state. It is these three that I shall mainly have in mind in what follows, but nearly all of the points made about the relation between the religious and the political are meant to apply, to some extent, to any religion.

The equalitarian principle

The case for the equalitarian principle is more complicated than the case for the libertarian principle. The (or a) central premise of the former case is that if the state prefers one or more religions, its people might well find it hard to practice another, or would at least feel pressure to adopt or give preferential treatment to the (or a) religion favored by the state. The degree of pressure would tend to be proportional to the strength of governmental preference. That preference might be great enough to require a certain religious affiliation for holding a government job, or as minor as inviting clergy from only one religion to officiate at small, local ceremonies.

Any governmental religious preference for a particular religion, however, creates some tendency for greater power to accrue to the preferred religion, particularly if it is that of the majority. Even if the existence of certain disproportionate powers does not necessarily (or at least does not directly) restrict anyone's liberty, concentration of power in a religious group as such easily impairs democracy, in which citizens should have equal opportunities to exercise political power on a fair basis, and it may impair religious freedom in particular. Moreover, where a state establishes or prefers a given religion, we may anticipate (though it is perhaps not inevitable) that certain laws will significantly reflect the world view associated with that religion. These are among the reasons a free and democratic society should adopt the equalitarian principle. Even where the libertarian principle is respected, the equalitarian principle is needed to protect citizens against governmental discrimination.

The neutrality principle

As to the rationale for the neutrality principle, recall that religious liberty, broadly conceived, includes the freedom to reject religious views. If the state shows preference for religious institutions as such (or for the practice of religion in general), there may well be pressure to adopt a religion, and quite possibly discrimination against those who do not. To be sure, some kinds of state preference for religious people or institutions as such are consistent with religious liberty; hence, the neutrality principle cannot be simply derived from the libertarian principle. There are many domains of state preference for the religious as such. Mandatory prayer sessions in public schools, religious exemptions from combat duty, and religious eligibility requirements for adopting children are examples. Other possibilities are tax deductions given to people sending their children to church-supported schools but not to people sending them to secular private schools, preference (other things equal) in filling government posts ordinarily earned by competition on the basis of merit alone, and statutory roles for religious institutions or their representatives in government, as in the case of the Archbishop of Canterbury in England.[6]

Preferences of the sort indicated may tend toward political domination by the religious, even if in principle the pressures created by those preferences could be prevented from causing it. Thus, even if there is protection from both religious tyranny and discriminatory exclusions of some disfavored groups on religious grounds, governmental preference of the religious as such is likely to give them advantages that threaten a proper democratic distribution of political power. It can also reduce the level of free *exercise* of liberty, as opposed to its mere legal *scope*. The more difficult it is to exercise a liberty—as where non-religious people must make themselves conspicuous by abstaining from reciting the Pledge of Allegiance—the less we tend to do it.[7]

There are, however, further reasons for a liberal democracy to adopt the neutrality principle even if such a society did not have to be committed to protecting the freedom not to be religious. (These reasons may of course also provide support for the equalitarian principle.) Once the state favors the religious over the non-religious, at least three problems arise.

First. Where there is a majority affiliation, the views and even the interests of this group are likely to dominate legislation and policy affecting religion, sometimes to the detriment of religious minorities, for instance in the treatment of religious schools and the celebration of major events, such as inaugurations and holidays.

Second. Religious disagreements are likely to polarize government, especially regarding law and policy concerning religion, say requirements for conscientious objector status or, at the institutional level, for tax exemption. Each religious group will tend to have its own conception not only of what constitutes a religion in the first place but also of what criteria a religious group must fulfill to receive exemptions or other benefits. Granted that secular disputes can also polarize, other things equal they have less tendency to do this. If ideological disputes, say between communism and fascism, seem exceptions to this, that may be in part because of how much an ideology can have in common with a religion. (The more like a religion it is, of course, the less other things are equal.) Secular disputes, as compared with religious ones, also tend to be resolvable without either side's making as fundamental concessions.

Third. If a government prefers the religious over the non-religious, it will tend, through the pronouncements and social policies that express that preference, to influence churches, and, in deciding what to promote in the religious sphere, to begin to set criteria for what counts as being religious in the sense that qualifies institutions for preference. Once there are benefits to be had, there will be stretching to meet the criteria for getting them. This is a likely way to much "entanglement" of the government in religious affairs.[8]

It might be argued that the only reason to avoid reducing the exercise, as opposed to the scope, of freedom in a democratic society is a commitment to fostering pluralism. But the distinction is not sharp: apart from a courageous few, making the exercise of a freedom costly shades into narrowing its scope. Moreover, quite independently of a commitment to fostering pluralism, a liberal democracy should avoid reducing the exercise of freedom, if only because diminutions in the exercise of freedom tend to lessen creativity both in the lives of individuals and in the solution of social problems.

A further ground for the neutrality principle is the ideal of equal treatment not solely among the religious but among citizens in general, an ideal that, like liberty, is an important element in a free and democratic society. Governmental preference for the religious as such is intrinsically unequal treatment of the religious and non-religious, however minor the resulting material differences may be. On balance, then, the neutrality principle seems required to guarantee protection from governmental favoritism, in the sense of preferential treatment of the religious over the non-religious. Even if this treatment does not involve discrimination in favor of one religious group, non-religious citizens will tend to *feel* it as discrimination and not as a legitimate expression of the will of a democratic majority. Freedom and democracy are best served by principles that keep the state from restricting *or* influencing religious institutions as such any more than is required for enacting laws and policies that are justified on non-religious grounds.

Religious Obligation and Political Conduct

As individuals living in a liberal democracy, we are less constrained than are governments and institutions by principles that restrict sociopolitical conduct. It is indeed arguable that a citizen in
such a society may properly vote or engage in other political conduct on any conscientiously chosen basis. But some of the same
grounds—including protection of religious liberty—that underlie
separation of church and state at the institutional level may, at the
individual level, warrant a measure of separation of religious and
secular considerations. I want to explore the extent to which this is
so.

Despite the connections between the institutional and individual levels and the bearing of liberal democratic theory on both, I
think it is instructive to begin not (as is common) with the implications of some liberal theory of the state for the conduct of citizens
or institutions but instead with the point of view of a morally up-
right religious citizen who wants to live in a free and democratic
society. Let us ask not what religious citizens should do if liberalism
is sound, but whether a version of liberalism can be reasonably
reached from a certain range of religious perspectives. My main
question in this section, then, is this: What should conscientious
religious citizens in a pluralistic society want in the way of protection of their own freedom and promotion of standards that express
respect for citizens regardless of their religious position?

Suppose that I am devoutly religious and that my religion implies much about how a good life is to be lived. I might subscribe
to the Ten Commandments and to Jesus' injunction to love our
neighbors as ourselves. I thus have far-reaching, religiously
grounded prima facie obligations relevant to my conduct as a citizen,
and I might try to lead my day-to-day life with such religious standards in mind.[9] May I, as a conscientious citizen, pursue these obligations as vigorously as possible within the limits of the law? This is
a plausible view; but let us go beyond taking the law as our baseline,
since the law may be either unjustifiably restrictive or unwarrantedly
permissive. May I, as a conscientious citizen, pursue my religious
obligations so far as possible within the limits of my moral rights?
An affirmative answer to this second question also seems plausible,

at least if the issue is *moral* propriety; for if I were violating anyone else's moral rights, I would presumably be going beyond mine.

There are, I shall argue, moral considerations bearing on this issue that go beyond the question of what we have a right to do. There are ideals of moral virtue that require of us more than simply acting within our moral rights. In particular, there are *ideals of civic virtue* that arguably derive from moral ideals (though I cannot try to do a derivation here) and demand of us more than simply staying within our rights. In setting out and defending this perspective, I shall first briefly consider the nature and dimensions of religious obligation. I shall then sketch a partial conception of civic virtue, with liberal democracy in mind as the context of its exercise. And against that background I shall suggest how civic virtue and religious obligation can be reasonably integrated.

Grounds and dimensions of religious obligation

Religious obligation has at least five kinds of evidential grounds. In describing these, and indeed in discussing religious obligation in relation to civic virtue, I shall be thinking above all of the Hebraic-Christian tradition; but the points that emerge will apply, to varying degrees, to other traditions, including, to some extent, certain non-theistic religious traditions. The five sources I have in mind are (1) scripture; (2) non-scriptural religious authority, especially that of the clergy, but including the authority of the relevant community, such as the theological community if there is one; (3) tradition, which often implies presumptions regarding one's religious obligations and may in some cases be quite authoritative; (4) religious experience; and (5) natural theology, for instance the philosophical kind illustrated by Thomas Aquinas's famous five arguments for the existence of God, each proceeding from non-religious premises. Divine command is of course distinct from any of these sources of religious obligation, but I am supposing for the sake of argument that *evidences* of it in human life will come from one of the sources. Several further comments are called for.

First, a source of religious obligation may require a kind of conduct directly—as by commanding it in the way God is biblically described as having commanded the actions that Moses singled out in the Ten Commandments—or indirectly, as where Jesus exemplifies a kind of conduct and the text presents it as incumbent on us. Second, there are both direct and indirect obligations that go with a general commitment to an institutional religion; these include both *religious obligations* in the narrow sense, for example to engage in certain rituals, and *obligations of a religion* (some of which are non-religious in content), such as Christians' obligations to contribute to charity. Third, there are special obligations, such as those arising from what is revealed in a religious experience, which may fall not only on the person in question, chiefly the one having the experience, but perhaps also on those addressed in it. My whole family might, for example, be singled out in a religious experience of mine and might acquire a religious or other obligation through what I credibly report as revealed to me. Fourth, there are what might be called *supererogations*—types of conduct that are highly desirable (and so are often presented in a favorable light) but not obligatory: they represent going beyond the call of duty.[10] All four cases concern me, but it will not in general be necessary to address them separately.

It is also important, in discussing religious obligation, to distinguish its grounds from its content—its basis as contrasted with the conduct it requires. An obligation can have religious grounds without having religious content, such as theological or liturgical content. This is illustrated by the non-theological commandments among the Ten, for instance the prohibition of bearing false witness: here a principle with secular content is presented as based on religious grounds. If, however, we take this distinction to imply that we should not in any circumstances call the obligations imposed by those commandments religious, we lose contact with an important constraint: an obligation whose non-fulfillment is religiously criticizable is to that extent a religious obligation. It is an obligation *of* a religion, even if not an obligation having religious content.

We should also distinguish those religious obligations that are *aligned* with non-religious ones, such as the obligation not to murder, from those that are religious in content (and from those that are neither), and I will generally use the term 'religious obligation' to refer to obligations that are clearly grounded wholly or primarily in a religious source.[11] I leave open whether these must be objective, externally grounded obligations, as opposed to being, say, reasonably *believed,* from the point of view of a person's religious commitments and relevant non-religious beliefs, to be objective obligations. This leaves open the possibility that there can be religious obligations even if the associated religious presuppositions (such as theism itself) should be mistaken, but it does not force us to attribute to a people just any religious obligation they believe they have, nor to adopt any specific account of the nature and force of any subjective religious obligations there may be. There are, for at least the religious traditions most important to this essay, internal standards for responsibly determining when one has a religious obligation.

The mutual independence of religious sources of obligation

It seems clear that the five sources of religious obligation I have listed are, though historically interdependent, logically independent, in the sense that "endorsement," by any one of them, of a proposition favoring some conduct does not entail its endorsement by any other source among the five.[12] Their close historical association may tend to hide their logical independence, but the latter is of great importance. It suggests the possibility both of conflicts between the sources and of mutual support among them. The support that a source gives to an action may be merely partial. First, one or more sources may provide some degree of support for a kind of conduct, yet not imply the strong conclusion that conduct of this kind is obligatory. Second, two or more sources may be jointly but not individually sufficient: no one of them implies that action of the kind in question is obligatory, but, taken together, they do imply this. Third, we may have *obligational overdetermination*: two or more sources may each be sufficient to imply an obligation. It should not be surprising, then, if some religious obligations are stronger than others, whether because two or more sources coincide in requiring the act in question as against one source prohibiting it, or because one source is clearer or more weighty than some other single source. This differential strength of religious obligations is indeed reflected in the way they are sometimes presented in scriptures.[13]

Suppose, then, that multiple religious sources can converge in favoring the same obligatory behavior, such as giving to the poor. Suppose further that a religious obligation can be aligned with a secular one—one that is secularly grounded (which in principle could also have religious content, since one might, for example, promise to pray with someone and thereby have a moral reason, based on a duty of fidelity, to do a religious deed). We should now expect that there is sometimes not only a *plurality of different obligational grounds* for a kind of conduct, but also religiously and secularly *mixed obligational overdetermination*, the kind that occurs when there are both sufficient religious reasons *and* sufficient secular reasons for a kind of conduct, for instance truth-telling. Logically, neither the religious nor the secular ground is necessarily stronger than the other, either evidentially or motivationally. Genetically, neither kind need be prior. Some people learn at least some of their moral principles first through religious education and later see a secular rationale for them; other people first learn at least some of their moral principles through secular education and later see a religious rationale for them.

Connections among religious and secular sources

If we think of the Hebraic-Christian tradition, it is clear that there is much overlap between religiously and secularly grounded obligations. This tradition is not opposed to taking secular grounds seriously, nor even to looking to them for purposes of, say, better understanding the conduct required by both sets of grounds, or of enhancing one's motivation to produce that conduct. Granted that a person's faith can and should inform aspects of secular life, including especially the treatment of other people, reflective secular living can also lead to enhanced understanding of one's faith. Taken together with the multiplicity and independence of religious grounds, their internal diversity, and the unclarity (in some cases) of their bearing on conduct, this complicated, mutually enriching relation between religious and secular grounds has important implications. Two implications in particular concern me: one regarding religious individuals themselves, the other concerning their relations to their non-religious fellow citizens.

Consider rational individuals who are aware (as are many educated people) of the independence of religious sources, of the overlap between religious and secular obligations, and of the extent of

religious diversity within and, especially, among traditions, both religious and non-religious. Should we not expect such individuals to
seek confirmation of, or at least mutual support among, some of
these justificatory sources, as they bear on judgments of far-reaching
obligation? Some of those judgments, after all, are controversial or
unclear or difficult to live up to; hence, mutual support of a judgment by sources to which one is committed should normally be felt
to be at once confirmatory, clarifying, and motivating. That support
can increase the likelihood that the judgment is true, clarify what it
means, and add to one's motivation to act on it. Furthermore, if the
support includes secular considerations, there is the special satisfaction of being able to maintain that one's religious perspective leads
to a truth that can be appreciated independently of it—and that can
perhaps be a route by which others may join one, from outside one's
tradition, in some project that this truth supports.

My suggestion, then, is that mature, rational, religious people
living in circumstances like those of a contemporary liberal democracy will seek at least a measure of reflective equilibrium among
their beliefs and attitudes grounded in religious sources of obligation
and, in some cases, among those elements *and* beliefs and attitudes
which they hold or find plausible, that they take to be grounded in
secular sources. Roughly, this effort is a search for a reflective cognitive balance in which the elements in question—chiefly one's beliefs, attitudes, and desires—are mutually consistent and, so far as
possible, mutually supportive.

The more rational we are, and the more complicated the moral
issues we face, the wider the equilibrium we are likely to seek. The
equilibrium may, though it need not, extend to theology, ethical
theory, and even scientific considerations. Thus, preferring to use
one's resources reserved for charity to support an orphanage over a
symphony might fit best with one's religious commitments, moral
priorities, and scientific sense of how to strengthen the social fabric,
whereas the thought of contributing to a candidate who favors most
of one's sociopolitical policies but is also stingy regarding foreign
aid may produce an ambivalence that precludes reaching reflective
equilibrium in making a contribution.

In the social arena, a mature, rational, religious person is likely to be sensitive not only to overlapping moral views but to moral and other disagreements that have at least potential religious significance. It is likely to seem quite appropriate in such cases to seek common ground with fellow citizens with whom one disagrees in major moral or sociopolitical matters. Perhaps one's view is supported by secular grounds that people of any religious persuasion can accept, even if appealing to those grounds means revising some aspect of one's own outlook. Indeed, I may find that I should revise something in my religious view: after all, once I take seriously the possibility of my religious sources yielding mutually conflicting results, I will be a fallibilist about my views of my religious obligations. I will recognize the possibility of making errors in identifying or interpreting them, particularly if I must rely on authorities in doing so—sometimes on authorities who themselves need labored interpretation. Their writings and sermons, for instance, may be complex, metaphorical, or ambiguous.

I may, to be sure, feel very confident of some particular religious obligation, such as the obligation to try to love others and to spread the word of God among those who have not received it; the sense of my fallibility need not in all cases reduce my confidence. But this sense may still moderate—and it certainly bears on—what I should be willing to *do* on the basis of that confidence.

Fallibilism about one's conception of one's religious obligations is particularly significant, I think, where two conditions hold: first, the issue is what we are morally permitted or obligated to do in *non*-religious matters, and second, one can find no good secular ground for one's religiously based view. For although no secular reason need be expected for engaging in the special rites and rituals appropriate within a religious community, there is something of a presumption that such reasons may be found for our *general* moral obligations, including obligations to prevent or promote certain kinds of social conduct. I shall return to this issue.[14] For now, it is enough to have argued that both an effort to achieve reflective equilibrium on certain important matters and an attitude of fallibilism are appropriate to mature, rational practitioners of a religion for which, as is typical, there are multiple, independent, and sometimes unclear or ambiguous sources of authority regarding human conduct.[15]

Civic Virtue and Religious Conviction

The partial picture that I have painted of a mature, rational, religious person surely indicates some of the makings of civic virtue. But before pursuing the question of how religious and civic ideals are connected, let us ask what sort of thing constitutes civic virtue in a liberal democracy (which I shall assume is embedded in a just state).

Suppose one has a feature of character strongly disposing one to obey the law, or at any rate to obey just laws. Is this sufficient for having civic virtue? I think not. One would not thereby do any charitable deeds and, far from participating in the life of society, could largely shun it. Virtuous citizens—certainly those in the Hebraic-Christian tradition—try to contribute in some way to the welfare of others, including others beyond their immediate community. In a society that is complex, pluralistic, and so, inevitably, somewhat divided, civic virtue implies trying to take reasonable positions on important issues, voting, discussing problems with others, and more. Civic virtue in a liberal democracy implies a degree of responsible political participation.

A liberal democracy by its very nature resists using coercion, and prefers persuasion, as a means to achieve cooperation. What we are persuaded to do, by being offered reasons for it, we tend to do autonomously and to identify with; what we are compelled to do we tend to resent doing. Thus, when there must be coercion, liberal democracies try to justify it in terms of considerations—such as public safety—that any rational adult citizen will find persuasive and can identify with.[16] This is one reason why religious grounds alone are not properly considered a sufficient basis of coercion even if they happen to be shared by virtually all citizens. If fully rational citizens in possession of the relevant facts cannot be persuaded of the necessity of the coercion—as is common where that coercion is based on an injunction grounded in someone else's religious scripture or revelation—then from the point of view of liberal democracy, the coercion lacks an adequate basis. A liberal state exists in good part to accommodate a variety of people irrespective of their special preference for one kind of life over another; it thus allows coercion only where necessary to preserve civic order and not simply on the basis of majority preference.[17]

As advocates for laws and public policies, then, and especially for those that are coercive, virtuous citizens will seek grounds of a kind that any rational adult citizen can endorse as sufficient for the purpose. Virtuous citizens tend to be motivated in this direction in proportion to the burdensomeness of the coercion, for instance to be more concerned with the rationale for military conscription than with the basis for requiring drivers to be licensed.

The suggested adequacy condition for justifying coercion implies intelligibility of a certain kind (allowances being made for technical considerations in some cases); more to the point here, it implies secularity. I hasten to add that if civic virtue does imply such a search, that is not in the least to suggest any attempt to abandon religious grounds or even to abstract from them as potential evidence or motivation. This brings us to the question of how civic virtue is related to religious commitment.

Civic virtue, religious commitment, and moral obligation

I have already suggested that there is in fact a great deal of overlap between the content of certain religiously based obligations and that of widely recognized secularly based moral obligations, and I think that there is substantial overlap with respect to major moral principles, such as those prohibiting murder, assault, injustice (including political oppression), theft, and dishonesty and those requiring some degree of beneficence toward other people, say in cases where one can help others with no significant sacrifice to oneself (this conception of moral overlap is similar to Rawls's idea of an overlapping consensus, though that notion includes sociopolitical principles as well as basic moral ones). I now want to go further than the overlap thesis regarding religiously based obligations and widely recognized secularly based moral obligations. I begin with a conception of God that seems at least implicit in what we might loosely call standard Western theism: I have in mind chiefly Christianity, Judaism, and Islam, the Abrahamic religions, as they are sometimes called; and I am speaking from the point of view of natural theology,

_⸅ available to any rational informed inquirer, not the theol-
⸗y of any particular religion.[18]

If we assume a broadly Western theism, we can take God to be
omniscient, omnipotent, and omnibenevolent. Might we not, then
(at least given this set of divine attributes), expect God to structure
us free rational beings and the world of our experience so that there
is a (humanly accessible) secular path to the discovery of moral
truths, at least to those far-reaching ones needed for the kind of
civilized life we can assume God would wish us to live? Let me try
to develop this idea.

It must first be granted that if God has created an ambiguous
world in which evil looms so large that even many theists are
tempted to conclude that this sorry world cannot be created by *God*,
then it would seem possible that there is no secular path to moral
truths. But it is one thing for God to test us and provide conditions
for our freely choosing to become children of God; it is quite another thing to make it virtually impossible for those who do not so
choose, even to be moral in non-theological matters.[19] Why would
God compound the incalculable loss suffered by rejecting one's Cre-
ator with the impossibility of even discovering how one should be-
have in the absence of such a supreme authority who can guide
one's daily life?

If the freedom preserved by the religious ambiguity of the
world is so valuable, should we not expect God to provide for access
to rational standards, discoverable by secular inquiry, for the proper
exercise of that freedom, as opposed to its abuse or waste in immoral, wrong-headed, or ignorant behavior? If God cares enough
about us not to compel us toward theism but instead to allow our
free choice or rejection of it, would it not seem that we would be
equipped with standards for the use of our freedom in the ways
appropriate to God's creatures? Even if one thinks that much of our
misfortune is a result of our own sin, one might reasonably expect
that God would not allow us to be deprived of the minimum standards required to understand our own wrongdoing and use our freedom to rectify it.

Moreover, if one thinks, as a great many theists do, that natural
theology yields a rational, non-religious route to religious truths, it
is reasonable to expect that there might be a counterpart secular

route to at least some basic moral truths.[20] It seems altogether appropriate that, in ethics as in religion, God should provide more than one path to truths essential for living a good life. The existence of multiple paths to a truth increases the likelihood of our finding it; the availability of many independent grounds for a truth makes it more likely that we will believe it with conviction and act on it when the going gets hard. Furthermore, if there is already a plurality of grounds for some major theological propositions and, in a different way, for some important theoretical conclusions in science, and if plurality in those domains is suggestive of God's provision for our discovering, in our individual ways, genuine religious and scientific truths, why should there not also be plurality with respect to grounds for major ethical truths?

Even if one does not agree that, given standard Western theism, we should expect there to be accessible, adequate, secular reasons for major moral principles, one may well grant (on other grounds) that there are such reasons. I believe that there are. I cannot show this here, but there is one general consideration that is highly suggestive. Suppose, as is widely held, that moral properties are in a certain way based on natural ones (supervene on them, in a terminology common in ethical theory), roughly in the sense that the moral properties of a person or an act are possessed by it in virtue of its natural properties: roughly, its factual (descriptive) ones, the kind ascertainable by scientific procedures, including ordinary observations of behavior. A person is honest, say, in virtue of a tendency to tell the truth (for an appropriate range of motivating reasons), and an act is obligatory, for instance, in virtue of being an avoidance of running over a child; and if a person is morally good, then so is any other person (e.g., a perfect clone) who is exactly similar in natural properties, such as psychological make-up taken to include intentions to treat people in certain ways, dispositions to share, aversions to fighting with others, and so forth.[21] Now, if there are natural properties determining moral properties, it is reasonable to think that in principle we can discover the presence of moral properties through discovering the presence of natural properties on which they depend. Natural properties are (as normally—and non-skeptically—conceived) accessible to secular reason.

To be sure, it could be that we are sometimes unable to tell

what moral properties a person or act has even when we know that
the person or deed has certain natural properties and these are in fact
the ones that underlie the former. We may not know this latter fact.
A psychological basis of deceitfulness, for instance, need not wear its
moral significance on its sleeve. It might be a special weakness that
only careful inquiry can show to be a producer of the moral defect
we call *deceitfulness*. We could, then, lack an appropriate principle
for connecting the former with the latter. But this does not in general happen: if you have a thorough knowledge of my personality,
views, and motives conceived non-morally, you are in an excellent
position to discern my moral character. We also have a good sense
of what *sorts* of natural properties are relevant to moral decisions, for
instance their properties affecting people's pleasure and pain, freedom of movement, and human capacities.[22] We know, for instance,
that equality of effort and output are relevant to the justice of remu-
neration, that being truthful with people is essential to treating them
with respect, and that brutality to children makes them suffer un-
justly and tends to make them abusive themselves, thereby continuing the infliction of suffering.

On the assumption that for major moral principles, there are
secular reasons sufficient to warrant accepting them (a possibility
that, incidentally, does not depend on the supervenience just hy-
pothesized as supporting it) we can appreciate a further connection
between the conception of God as omniscient and omnibenevolent
and the possibility of a rational secular path to moral truths—*any*
cogent argument, including an utterly non-religious one, for a moral
principle *is* in effect a good argument for (1) God's knowing that
conclusion—since God knows all truths—and hence, presumably,
for (2) God's wishing or requiring conformity to it. How could
God, conceived as omniscient and omnibenevolent, not require, or
at least wish, our conformity to a true moral principle?[23] It may turn
out that the theological significance of some moral arguments may
be at least as great as the moral significance of some theological
arguments. If, for instance, there are sound arguments for pacifism
or at least the position that only purely defensive wars are permissible, then a theology that represents God as commanding conquest
for the faith is mistaken.

I should think, moreover, that in some cases, good secular arguments for moral principles may be *better* reasons to believe those principles to be divinely enjoined than theological arguments for the principles, based on scripture or tradition. For the latter arguments seem (even) more subject than the former to cultural influences that may distort scripture or tradition or both; more vulnerable to misinterpretation of religious or other texts or to their sheer corruption across time and translation; and more liable to bias stemming from political or other non-religious aims. Granting, then, that theology and religious inspiration can be sources of ethical insight, we can also reverse this traditional idea: one may sometimes be better off trying to understand God through ethics than ethics through theology.[24]

Theo-ethical equilibrium

If these considerations from philosophical theology and ethical theory are sound, then civic virtue on the part of the religious should embody a commitment to *theo-ethical equilibrium*—a rational integration between religious deliverances and insights and, on the other hand, secular ethical considerations. Thus, a seemingly sound moral conclusion that goes against one's scriptures or one's well-established religious tradition should be scrutinized for error; a religious demand that appears to abridge moral rights should be studied for such mistakes as misinterpretation of what it requires, errors in a translation of some supporting text, and distortion of a religious experience apparently revealing the demand; a major moral principle derived from only one of the five sources of religious obligation should, in many cases, be tested against one or more of the other four and perhaps also against some secular source. Given the conception of God as omniscient, omnipotent, and omnibenevolent, the possibility of theo-ethical equilibrium is to be expected, and a mature, conscientious theist who cannot reach it should be reluctant or unwilling to support coercive laws or public policies on a religious basis that cannot be placed in that equilibrium.[25]

If we take a commitment to theo-ethical equilibrium to be (or at least to merit being) a major element in the civic virtue of the religious, are we deifying reason? I think not. Notice that although secular reason can lead to modifying one's religious views, religious considerations can also lead to revision of one's secular moral views. This applies especially to moral theories, but it extends even to "intuitive" moral judgments. Moreover, a commitment to seeking theo-ethical equilibrium leaves open whether one gives either kind of reason evidential priority or any other kind of precedence. The precedence of either one, however, is not license to ignore the other: a conscientious religious person aware of the relationships outlined here should not in general approve of any deed that is either morally or theologically impermissible.

A commitment to seeking theo-ethical equilibrium may be thought to split the self into religious and secular personae,[26] but it need not, and it can have the opposite effect. The intelligibility of separate grounds for action does not require different agents or subagents to grasp those grounds. Such intelligibility does not even imply different obligations to act on the separate grounds, as opposed to a single obligation with a plurality of supporting reasons. An action's being supported by two different kinds of grounds can indeed be a good occasion to connect those grounds as allied considerations. Disparate grounds may even be merged into a unified point of view, especially when theo-ethical equilibrium is achieved or, where it is not, when the grounds support the same or complementary actions. Moreover, each of several disparate grounds may be embraced from the standpoint of the others, as where secular benevolence is a fulfillment both of divine command and of a secular ethical commitment. This benevolence may issue in both individual acts of charity and a national policy of foreign aid.

For some religious outlooks, a commitment to seeking theo-ethical equilibrium, or even to the aspect of it that requires only seeking secular as well as religious grounds for major moral principles, may seem to go against the view that the whole of one's life must be devoted to doing God's will.[27] On two plausible assumptions, even this view can be accommodated by the position I am suggesting as a way of harmoniously combining the religious and the secular in a wide range of moral matters. The first assumption is that a property—such as that of being commanded by God—can appear to human intelligence in more than one guise, say in a Kantian guise as the property of befitting the dignity of persons or in an agapistic guise as the property of being appropriate to loving treatment of others. The second assumption is that if God either has ordained the coincidence of the property of being commanded by God with a property appearing in a secular guise, or has at least allowed us to discern the equivalence of the two or, minimally, to grasp the reasonableness of taking the property appearing in a secular guise as an adequate basis of action, then our being guided in our actions by the property in its secular guise is not irreverent. If, for instance, God has created me so that I grasp the dignity of other people as dictating just treatment of them, and I am motivated by that to treat them justly, then my doing so on that basis is not irreverent.

We may go further. If the property that I am morally responding to *is* that of being commanded by God, then even if I were a non-theist my conduct would be—unconsciously—reverent. If I can *conceive* my acting justly as also doing God's will, then from a religious point of view, so much the better; and nothing stops me from so conceiving it even if I am independently motivated by the moral sense of dignity as demanding justice. If the world that God has created exhibits divine will in a multiplicity of guises, why should I not appreciate that will in the variety of God's creation and allow those aspects of it that attract my rational allegiance to contribute to my motivation to be moral?

It should also be stressed that reason itself can be considered a gift from God and thereby divinely sanctioned for our use. Furthermore, even divine commands about its use—such as to love God with all one's mind—must be carried out using the very faculty they are to regulate. A certain autonomy of reason in governing human life is presupposed in any religious perspective. Extending a good measure of that autonomy to the ethical and religious domains seems consonant with piety.

The very notion of civic virtue, as contrasted with religious virtue, suggests that secular reason will play a major role in the former. One reaction would be to say that, if so, then the deeply religious are within their rights in rejecting the obligation to strive for civic virtue as understood here. My response to this is that they *may* be within at least their religious rights; but that depends on the very issue we are discussing: on what implications their overall religious view has for the treatment of other people, especially those outside their religious community. Thomas Aquinas's emphasis on natural law, and indeed Jesus' emphasis on loving one's neighbors, on non-violence, and on forgiveness, would suggest that civic virtue, especially when taken as embodying a commitment to theo-ethical equilibrium, should not (from within at least the major Christian traditions) be rejected. If, on the other hand, the question is whether we are within our moral rights in rejecting the proposed ideal of civic virtue so conceived, I would say that the answer is not clear. A major second-order moral obligation that we all seem to have is to take (first-order) moral obligations and principles seriously and to seek accommodation with those with whom we are obligated to live in peace despite our disagreements, whether they are outside our own religious tradition or within it.

Suppose, however, that we would be within both our moral and our religious rights in rejecting this ideal of civic virtue. Is doing so morally desirable, and would it be morally virtuous? My answer to both questions is negative. Whether, from a religious point of view, this answer is reasonable depends on the conditions for achieving theo-ethical equilibrium within that point of view and on what sorts of principles support giving such equilibrium a serious place in one's sociopolitical conduct. I have already suggested that given omniscience, omnipotence, and omnibenevolence as elements in the conceptions of God prevalent in standard Western theism, a major factor in the equilibrium should be good secular arguments for moral principles. To connect samples of these arguments with any specific religion is too large a task to undertake here. But the next section will suggest some principles of conscience that commend themselves both as elements in civic virtue and as prima facie guides to achieving theo-ethical equilibrium.

Some Principles and Practices of Civic Virtue

Given the way in which a virtue ethics is often contrasted with an ethics of rules or principles, it may seem odd to speak of *principles* of virtue. But first, I am not here endorsing virtue ethics overall, and second, principles may have a major role even in a virtue ethics. Even if traits are morally fundamental, we can formulate principles on the basis of observing the conduct of virtuous agents in sufficiently diverse circumstances. A habitually virtuous agent will often act on principles so derived.[28]

Secular rationale

The first principle I want to discuss—which, in earlier work, I have called the *principle of secular rationale*—says that one has a prima facie obligation not to advocate or support any law or public policy that restricts human conduct, unless one has, and is willing to offer, adequate secular reason for this advocacy or support (say for one's vote). If, for instance, I want to advocate mandatory periods of prayer or meditation in public schools, I should have adequate secular reason for this, such as its being educationally and psychologically essential for the nation's youth. If my only reason is to promote my own or other religious ideals, then I would not satisfy this principle. I would be moving toward reducing the freedom of students who would like to avoid such sessions without an adequate rationale independent of my own religious commitments. This might not disturb me insofar as I think of what I am doing as essential for the spiritual well-being of students. But if, for example, I imagine being forced to observe certain dietary laws or to dress in a certain style because another religion gains a majority and makes it legally binding, I may begin to see the advantages of adhering to the principle of secular rationale in matters of coercive law or public policy. Five additional points of clarification are in order immediately.

First, most laws and public policies do restrict human conduct to some extent, and the more restrictive the laws or policies in question, the stronger the relevant obligation. It is useful here to distinguish *primary coercion* and *secondary coercion*. The first requires a particular action, such as paying taxes or submitting to inoculation. The second occurs in at least two ways. It may operate on the basis of the former, as where one's tax payments—already legally required—are spent partly in ways one disapproves of, so one is in a sense funding something against one's will. Secondary coercion may also be only conditional, as where it applies in circumstances that citizens may avoid, say by deciding not to drive and so avoid being forced to go through the process of licensing. Other things equal, primary coercion is more in need of justification than is secondary coercion.

Second, my main concern is what I propose to call *positive restrictions*—roughly, coercion or restriction of the conduct of ordinary citizens—as opposed to *negative restrictions*, which are roughly the coercion or restriction of the enforcement of positive restrictions, chiefly by governmental or institutional officials. Negative restrictions are second order, being restrictions of restrictions, and they amount to liberalizations. Restricting the government's power to investigate individuals, for instance, enhances individual liberty. For enhancing liberty, a free and democratic society does not ordinarily need to require special reasons; nurturing liberty is one of its constitutive purposes. But consider restricting government from investigating individuals even in legitimate law enforcement; here liberalization might produce exploitation of some individuals by others and thus produce restrictions of freedom that would be justified only if an adequate secular reason can be given for them. Negative and positive restrictions are, then, interconnected, and this must be kept in mind even though the former will not be discussed further here.

Third, the secular rationale principle seems to have some force even widened to apply to non-restrictive laws and public policies (those that, like laws enabling a certain kind of agreement to be a legal contract, impose no significant positive restrictions); but these less troublesome cases do not concern me here. It would be quite enough to speak adequately to those issues involving religion and politics that raise questions of substantially burdensome coercion, such as the issue of state-sponsored school prayer.

Fourth, I am taking a secular reason as roughly one whose normative force, i.e., its status as a prima facie justificatory element, does not evidentially depend on the existence of God (or on denying it) or on theological considerations, or on the pronouncements of a person or institution *qua* religious authority.[29] Roughly, this is to say that a secular reason is a ground that enables one to know or have some degree of justification (roughly, evidence of some kind) for a proposition, such as a moral principle, independently of having knowledge of, or justification for believing, a religious proposition. Evidential independence of God on the part of reasons does not imply independence of God in general.[30] There are of course moral skeptics who think there *are* no adequate reasons for moral judgments, but I assume here that this is not so, that, for instance, an adequate secular reason for making murder and rape punishable is that they are morally wrong, serious threats to the security of society, and require legal punishability at least on grounds of adequate deterrence. Not every category of moral principle is so close to being uncontroversial among civilized people, and there are of course disagreements on significant matters of detail, such as the appropriate severity of punishments. But similar moral principles basic to a liberal legal structure can be seen (by non-skeptics) to be adequately justified by secular reasons concerning enslavement, theft, fraud, and many other behaviors that every free and democratic society prohibits by law.[31]

Fifth, I am taking a prima facie obligation to be one that provides a reason for action strong enough to justify the action in the absence of conflicting considerations, but is also liable to being overridden by one or more such considerations. Among the overriders of the obligation to have and be willing to offer secular reason are special circumstances in which secrecy is necessary, as where one would be in serious danger if certain people knew what legislation or candidate one was supporting. (Other overriders will be considered later.)[32]

If, given God's omniscience, omnipotence, and omnibenevolence, there is as much reason to expect alignment between religiously well-grounded and secularly well-grounded moral standards as I have suggested, then following the principle of secular rationale may be reasonably expected not to put a religious person (at least in the tradition of standard Western theism) into disequilibrium except where there is an error, for instance where at least one of the two sets of grounds is erroneous (say, embodying a false premise or an invalid inference). If, for example, a standard of punishment is irresolvably inconsistent with divinely required mercifulness, then perhaps revenge has been confused with retribution.

One might reply that "If people are told that, at least in the absence of adequate secular reasons, they should not rely on religious beliefs to vote for candidates who will protect animals, this is a serious constraint on the free exercise of their religion. As a modern statement of the Presbyterian Church (U.S.A.) puts it, '[I]t is a limitation and denial of faith not to seek its expression in both a personal and a public manner . . .' "[33] But even apart from my point that the civic obligation expressed in the principle of secular rationale is compatible with a right to do otherwise, this remark ignores the point that there are ways to enhance the protection of animals without appreciable restrictions of human conduct (nor is the example one in which there is any shortage of good secular reasons for advancing the relevant aim).

Suppose, however, that much money must be spent in enforcement and that many jobs are lost through the changes in the food sector of the economy, so that human conduct is significantly restricted, even if meat consumption remains legal. Then one might ask the religious voters in question whether they would accept comparable restrictions of their conduct, as well as similar job losses or mandatory shifts, on the basis of coercive legislation protecting the dandelion as a sacred species or prohibiting miniskirts and brief bathing suits as irreverent. The example is perhaps not realistic, at least for Western societies, but it helps to bring out the advantages that the principle of secular rationale offers for a plurality of peoples and faiths. It allows a great deal of "expression of faith in both a public and personal manner." Its limited restrictions of religious expression by some are protections of liberty for others—including the religious. Liberalism's constraints of some are liberations for others, and they are intended for the benefit of all.

The principle of secular rationale may be expected to have good effects for people *within* a religious tradition, for instance in different denominations and possibly even in the same denomination, as well as to facilitate good relations *between* different religious traditions and between religious and non-religious people. Intramural strife can be deadly. It seems less likely to occur where this principle is adopted.

Secular motivation

The second principle I suggest—which in earlier work I have called the *principle of secular motivation*—simply adds to the rationale principle a motivational condition. It says that one has a (prima facie) obligation to abstain from advocacy or support of a law or public policy that restricts human conduct, unless one is sufficiently *motivated* by (normatively) adequate secular reason, where sufficiency of motivation here implies that some set of secular reasons is motivationally sufficient, roughly in the sense that (a) this set of reasons explains one's action and (b) one would act on it even if, other things remaining equal, one's other reasons were eliminated.[34] Notice that since an argument can be tacitly religious without being religious in content, one might fail to adhere to at least the second of these principles even in offering arguments that on their face are neither religious nor fail to provide an adequate secular reason for their conclusion. Consider the genetic argument for the personhood of the zygote: roughly, the argument that since all the genetic information for its development into a person is present at conception, the zygote *is* a person at that point. It might be held that some people who offer this argument are not sufficiently motivated by the secular considerations cited in it, those just mentioned, and (quite apart from whether it is objectively sound) would not find the argument convincing apart from their underlying religious beliefs. They might, for example, think of the zygote as ensouled by God at the moment of its formation or might simply be brought up thinking of all human life as sacred.[35]

The principle of secular motivation may also be plausibly taken to rule out a certain kind of *anti*-religious motivation as properly necessary in coercive sociopolitical action. Imagine a scientific argument aimed at preventing creationism from being discussed in a public school science course: the secular considerations it cites might not be motivating, and if it is proposed from anti-religious motivation of a kind that does not count as secular, then even if it accords with the rationale principle, offering it does not accord with the motivation principle. Its proponent lacks a set of secular reasons that is both evidentially adequate and motivationally sufficient.[36]

Consider, by contrast, a case in which someone argues for a voucher system on the ground that parents, and especially religious ones, should be free to educate their children in academically adequate schools of their choice, including those that teach a particular religious point of view, and so should receive a voucher for each child, which can be used toward the costs of their children's attending any accredited school.[37] Here the *content* of the proposed legislation, unlike that of proposed restriction on abortion, includes a concern with religion and even envisages some likelihood of promoting its practice; but the *ground* given for the legislation is not intrinsically religious: one could support a voucher system on this ground without specially favoring the religious over, say, non-religious people who are simply dissatisfied with the general quality of public education, just as legislators can take account of the religiously based preferences of their constituents *as* their deep-seated preferences without thereby favoring the religious as such over other constituents.[38] If, however, pressing for a voucher system is to exhibit civic virtue as understood (in part) in terms of the principle of secular motivation, then some such secular consideration should be both (normatively) adequate and sufficiently motivating. If one's *only* reason for supporting vouchers is to promote the religious devotion of one's children (or other children), then even if one is expressing a kind of religious virtue, one is not exhibiting civic virtue.[39]

Granted, if there *is* an adequate secular reason for a policy, then no overall harm need be expected from the policy, and one might offer the reason as justifying one's conduct even if it does not motivate one. But let us apply the do-unto-others rule to that case: one would not like having a different religious group, with which one deeply disagrees, press for its religiously preferred policies solely for religious reasons of its own, even if a good secular reason could be offered. One's disapproving attitude may be modified only slightly where, although the secular reason motivates to some degree, it is inessential to determining support for the policies, which would have been promoted in its absence. We are especially likely to disapprove of the dominance of religious motivation if the policy or law in question is backed by severe punishments. As elsewhere in ethical matters, there can be a wrong way to do the right thing. The right way in cases of coercion must incorporate appropriate motivation.

The stress on secular reasons as evidential and motivational elements in civic virtue must not be taken to imply that such virtue requires no other constraints on appropriate reasons, such as prohibitions of racist grounds for public policy. This is not the place for an account of what makes certain reasons appropriate overall. Religious reasons, conceived (for instance) as reasons for human conduct that are ultimately grounded in God's nature or commands (or, at least from the point of view of religious persons, are rationally believed to be so grounded), are a major subject in their own right. There are some respects in which they are special in relation to liberal democracy even by contrast with other reasons—such as certain "intuitive" deliverances about other people—that are not accessible to any normal adult.[40] Here are some salient points.

First, the kinds of religious reasons of greatest concern in this essay are directly or indirectly taken to represent an infallible authority, in a sense implying that the propositions expressing them *must* be true.[41] A further implication many feel in such cases is that not to act on such considerations is a violation of divine command and is seriously wrong or even punishable by damnation.

Second, very commonly those who identify with what they regard as the ultimate divine source of religious reasons believe that anyone who does not identify with it is forsaken, damned, or in some other way fundamentally deficient. This disapproval is often enhanced or even inflamed by others' openly rejecting the relevant command or standard, as is common in, for example, sexual matters. Nor are religious people always consoled by knowledge that the disagreement with their religiously inspired views is respectful; this can be so even if they think those rejecting the views do so on the basis of *their* religious convictions. Following a false God—or misunderstanding the true one—can be worse than secular error.

Third, religious reasons often dictate practices that are distinctively religious in content (such as prayer) or intent (such as preserving a fetus on the ground that it is a gift from God), and therefore are plausibly seen in some cases as forcing others to observe a religious standard. This applies particularly where a religious consideration is used in favor of a practice for which there are no secular reasons persuasive to most reflective people not antecedently sympathetic on religious grounds, as in the case of most of the currently popular restrictions of abortion.

Fourth, for at least many religions—and commonly for what are plausibly called *cults*—rational, relevantly informed outsiders are unable to discern effective checks on certain possible tendencies for clergy (or, in some cases, votaries) to project, whether consciously

or otherwise, their own views or preferences into their interpretations of one or another authoritative religious source, including
even God.[42] In this case there is, in addition to the possibility of
some people's cloaking their prejudices with absolute authority, the
possibility that the views and motives of those who follow them lack
the minimal autonomy that citizens in a liberal democracy may hope
for in one another. Even if at the polling place the rule is one person,
one vote, it might be argued that people under the influence of cult
leaders or certain other kinds of dominating religious leaders may be
casting votes that not only fail to be independent but are also even
less open to reconsideration than most of the votes unduly influenced by secular figures.

Fifth, owing to some of these points (among others), religious
people often tend to be, in a way that is rare in secular matters,
highly and stubbornly passionate about the importance of everyone's
acting in accordance with religious reasons, and non-religious people often tend to be highly and stubbornly passionate about not
being coerced to do so. If many who are religious are vehemently
opposed to the sins of a multitude outside their fold, many who are
not religious are incensed at the thought of manipulation in the
name of someone else's non-existent deity.

Sixth, partly because religious liberty is a constitutive foundation (or at least a cogent rationale) for liberal democracy, citizens in
such a state are naturally and permissibly resentful about coercion by
religious factors (which may lead to restrictions of their specifically
religious behavior), in a way they are not permissibly resentful concerning coercion by, for instance, considerations of public health.

There may be other kinds of reasons to which each of these six
points (or close counterparts) applies individually; but if there are
any to which all of them apply, it is in a different way and is in any
event a good prima facie reason to impose similar restrictions on the
use of those reasons.[43]

It might still seem that motivation should not matter if the quality of one's reasons is good enough. This is a very difficult issue to
settle, if it can be settled. But I would stress that insofar as we are
thinking of the advocacy or other public behavior as supposed to be
action *from virtue*, we should look not just at what kind of act it is

and what can be said for it abstractly, but also at how it is grounded in the agent's *character.*[44] As Kant distinguished acting merely in conformity with duty and acting *from* duty, and Aristotle distinguished—as any virtue theorist should—actions that *express* virtue from those not virtuously performed but merely "in the right state," i.e., of the right type, we should distinguish actions from civic virtue and actions merely in conformity with it. There is no question that morally, one may, within one's rights, advocate a coercive course of action without being motivated by an adequate secular reason for that action; my contention is that to do so is not always consonant with civic virtue.

The principle of secular motivation, then, may be viewed as a *virtue principle*, whereas the principle of secular rationale is better viewed as a *justification principle* (and is the more important of the two for the ethics of citizenship). Action in accord with the latter, being supportable by adequate reason, may be considered to be justified. But this does not imply that it is virtuously performed—done from virtue—or indeed performed for any remotely admirable reason; nor does it imply that the agent is virtuous. Actions in accord with the principle of secular motivation, being sufficiently motivated by adequate reason, may be considered to be (at least to that extent) not only justified but also (civically) virtuous. Even if the agent is not habitually virtuous, the occasion in question is one on which an evidentially adequate set of reasons is also motivationally sufficient, and the action is to this extent virtuously performed.

It is a main contention of this essay that justification for sociopolitical action can be readily combined with motivation sufficient to realize it, and that where this combination does not occur, conscientious citizens should resist supporting coercive laws or policies even where they feel confident that they have an adequate rationale. The case for this *unity constraint*, as we might call it, roughly for integrating at least one evidentially adequate reason with motivation sufficient to produce action for that reason, will emerge more clearly in the light of considerations bearing on the voice with which good citizens should try to speak in debating issues of law and public policy.

Civic voice

The desirability of unifying our evidential and our motivational reasons may be more readily seen by reflecting on the difference between what we *say* to others and what we *communicate* to them. Saying 'I respect you' to someone may, for instance, be a cold acknowledgment of the person's rights and not at all reassuring. The motivation for saying it, and the tone with which it said—often produced by that motivation—are crucial to forming the actual message communicated.

The difference between what we literally say and what we communicate is particularly relevant to public debate on major human issues. We speak with different voices on different occasions and for different purposes. Even when they say the same thing, human voices can differ as radically as the timbres and resonances of different musical instruments sounding the same note; and, as it is the causal basis of those notes, not their pitch, that produces the quality of the instruments sounding them, with human speech it is the causal basis of what we say, including our motivation, not the content of what we say, that yields our voice.

Our voice is determined more by why and how we say what we do than by what we say, more by motive and manner than by content.[45] And we tend to listen for voicing as well as content: we try to hear more than just *what* people say, and quite commonly we accept—or reject—what others say because of how they voice it as well as because of what it is. Just criticism, delivered in a patronizing voice, is sometimes resisted precisely because of that voicing; a rejection of what we say, expressed impersonally and respectfully, may evoke fruitful revision of our view. Quite often, a disparity between content and voice, as when a scientific argument concerning abortion is religiously motivated and presented in a religious voice, can, though the proponent is entirely sincere, produce suspicion or resentment.

Part of civic virtue consists in having an appropriate *civic voice*; part of civic harmony in a framework of pluralism and disagreement consists in using that voice as the primary mode of communication in debating fundamental issues of citizenship. It need not be any citizen's only voice, not even for public argumentation and certainly not for self-expression. But it is achievable by any rational citizen committed to liberal democracy; and if I am right about the prospects for achieving theo-ethical equilibrium, then a civic voice is available, in part through adherence to the principle of secular motivation, to most rational religious people without compromise of their basic religious commitments.[46]

Is the mixed voice produced by combined religious and secular motivation consonant with civic virtue? It certainly may be: overdetermination need not produce discord; it can yield harmony. The cooperation of different elements can, moreover, produce a more powerful voice and, especially in a democracy, a more authoritative voice—a point worth noting both by those who would restrict political argument to publicly accessible considerations and by those who think secular reasons are not needed.

Here I differ from writers who (like Rawls) substantially restrict reliance on "comprehensive views" by citizens and, especially, judges and legislators.[47] My position allows (apart from special reasons to the contrary, such as the danger of producing violence or alienating an otherwise sympathetic audience) that comprehensive views, for instance a general set of moral and valuational standards, may figure crucially both evidentially and motivationally, and both in general public discussion and in advocacy and support of laws and public policies, provided (evidentially) adequate secular reasons play a sufficiently important role.[48] Furthermore, it can be helpful at certain points in public policy discussions to note what world view inspires one or how one's position does or does not accord with some major religious view. Discretion is needed here. What begins as candor and a search for a better understanding of the issues can easily degenerate into an unnecessary hardening of positions that might have been reconciled.[49]

The mutual integration of civic and religious virtues

There are saintly people whose actions may make it seem odd to take civic virtue to imply secular motivation and a mistake to conceive acting from civic virtue as grounded—at least in part— therein. Consider Mother Teresa. Doesn't her loving treatment of the sick manifest civic virtue? It certainly may. But to answer the question adequately we must distinguish civic virtue proper, as a *civically grounded* state of character, from civic virtue in a looser, behavioral sense: a *civically directed* disposition to do things having civic value. Similarly, we must distinguish action performed from civic virtue and, on the other hand, civically directed action. Virtues are best classified by their grounds, roughly the crucial elements of motivation and cognition that explain what the agent is doing in manifesting those elements of character, and why. Is the agent above all carrying out God's command, for instance, or giving aid to the destitute, or both? Virtues are not best classified in terms of a person's typical external conduct—good though that often is in indicating the presence of a virtue—but on the basis of how they motivate that conduct.

To see why virtues are best classified by reference to their grounds in the agent's beliefs and goals, recall that action which behaviorally conforms with virtue may stem from other sources, from prudence to treachery to dissembling to self-deception. Mother Teresa could be expected to have *both* religious reasons and secular motivation, such as simple human compassion, even if the virtue that she acts from in most of her daily conduct is religiously grounded devotion to others. The same person, moreover, may be differentially motivated by one of two compatible aims depending on the situation: at evening prayers, her charitable work might be spurred by a sense of divine command; at the moment of straining to lift a fainting child, by compassion. On my view, however, she has little if any moral *need* to exercise civic virtue in her charitable work. She is not promoting restrictive laws or policies; far from restricting people, her work restores and liberates them.

Nor do I claim that civic virtue is intrinsically better than religious virtue; they are good in different ways. Mother Teresa's charitable work is, however, perfectly compatible with her having civic virtue, and one can act from two virtues, just as one can act from two motives.[50] Civic virtue is needed above all where one is advocating or otherwise supporting laws or public policies that would restrict human freedom. Much of human life does not involve such conduct; much that does can be guided by cooperating religious and secular motives.

The principle of theo-ethical equilibrium

Given the importance of such cooperating religious and secular motives, it is appropriate to formulate a second-order principle that facilitates application of, and adherence to, the principles of secular rationale and motivation. This higher-order principle is based on the idea that there is much to be gained, intellectually and motivationally, from seeking theo-ethical equilibrium in deciding a wide range of important questions. For those who are religious, then (and possibly even as a heuristic principle for some who, though not religious, can think sympathetically and fruitfully in religious terms), I propose a *principle of theo-ethical equilibrium*: where religious considerations appropriately bear on matters of public morality or of political choice, religious people have a prima facie obligation—at least insofar as they have civic virtue—to seek an equilibrium between those considerations and relevant secular standards of ethics and political responsibility. I take this obligation to seek equilibrium to be strongest where support of a law or public policy that would restrict human conduct is in question, but I believe that some obligation may remain even apart from such cases.

Much is still left unspecified here. How readily should the bearing of religious considerations on the matter at hand be discernible in order for the obligation to seek theo-ethical equilibrium to become operative? How much effort should one expend in connection with decisions regarding law or public policy in order to discern whether there is any such bearing? And what ethical and political standards must one consider in relation to such decisions? A great deal could be said, but I leave the issue for another occasion. I would add, however, that one may seek a still wider equilibrium, for instance where the application of a moral standard to a concrete case requires a knowledge of many facts, say medical facts about the population needing help and sociological facts concerning their patterns of life. Here one may properly seek an equilibrium that yields a sociopolitical judgment which is at once morally and religiously sound and scientifically informed. It should be no surprise that a principle of virtue is not quantifiable and requires finding an Aristotelian mean between excess and deficiency.

Separation of Church and State as Addressed to the Church

My concern so far has been with governmental activities as they
affect religion and, even more, with standards of sociopolitical conduct appropriate to conscientious citizens in a free and democratic
society. But a full-blooded liberal theory of institutional separation
of the religious and the political has another component, also based
on ideals underlying liberal democracy. For many of the same reasons why the state should not interfere in religion, churches should
not interfere in government. The point is not legal or even constitutional. I am not suggesting, for example, that church donations to
political candidates must be illegal in a liberal democracy—though
presumably they should be *if* churches have tax-exempt status. My
point is that protection of religious liberty, and certainly of governmental neutrality toward religious institutions, is better served if,
normally, churches as such abstain from political action.

This political neutrality proposal goes somewhat beyond what
one would expect in the institutional counterparts of the principles
of secular rationale and secular motivation. For a church might, in
supporting a law or public policy, often both have and be sufficiently
motivated by a moral consideration bearing on a political issue. This
ecclesiastical moral engagement is surely desirable in a liberal democracy, and it is quite likely to occur if, in moral matters, churches
abide by an *institutional principle of theo-ethical equilibrium*, which says
that religious institutions, at least insofar as they are committed to
citizenship in a free and democratic society, have a prima facie obligation to seek such equilibrium in deciding to advocate or support
laws or public policies that restrict human conduct. This equilibrium
principle is a plausible candidate for a principle of institutional civic
virtue and is quite far-reaching.

A counterpart principle has some application to those secular
private institutions, such as colleges and universities with many religious faculty and students, for which it is appropriate to bring religious considerations into the relevant range of public policy
decisions. Serving the religious needs of faculty and students, for
example, even if done for secular reasons, can often be best achieved
if the activities by which it is accomplished are selected in part in
the light of reasoning that seeks a theo-ethical equilibrium. Consider

a decision concerning whether prayer should come into the commencement ceremony and, if so, how and with what sort of content. Here considerations drawn from the various religions represented among faculty and students are quite relevant, and they should be placed in equilibrium with such concerns as whether prayer, or a certain kind of prayer, would alienate or offend the non-religious people attending.

Supposing the equilibrium principle is sound, why is it not enough of a constraint to ask churches to adopt that principle in a liberal democracy? Why should we go beyond it to the suggested neutrality proposal, which calls not for theo-ethical equilibrium as a constraint on political conduct but for political neutrality on the part of churches? This is an important question on which liberals disagree among themselves, with only some of them taking the suggested step toward neutrality. Let us explore the matter.

Ecclesiastical neutrality

One possible ground for the neutrality proposal is that in their official institutional actions churches are commonly understood to be acting *as* religious institutions whose major concerns and bases of action are always religious and thus best not pursued in politics. That common understanding, however, has limited force when it does apply and, in any case, does not always apply. It is simply not true that religious institutions can properly have or be motivated only by religious reasons. For at least a great many churches, it can be quite proper both to take a moral position as such and to consider a moral conclusion as such to be sufficient for a political position. To be sure, a church conceivably could be committed to taking no moral positions as such but *only* as theologically derived. This, however, is not likely and seems inappropriate to at least the Hebraic-Christian tradition. I think it turns out, then, that we need a more fine-grained understanding of the proper role of churches in a free and democratic society than we can achieve either by construing them as governed in every detail by theological or religious considerations or by simply extending the rationale, motivation, and equilibrium principles to churches and perhaps to other institutions such as certain universities.

Let me tentatively suggest, as a partial solution to the problem of how best to conceive the role of churches in democratic politics, a *principle of ecclesiastical political neutrality*: in a free and democratic society, churches committed to being institutional citizens in such a society have a prima facie obligation to abstain from supporting candidates for public office or pressing for laws or public policies that restrict human conduct.[51] This principle applies not only to religious institutions as social entities but (if this is different) to their official representatives acting as such.[52] Even for churches not committed to citizenship in a liberal democracy, a case can be made that it would be good for them to recognize such an obligation of neutrality, but here I restrict attention to the former case. A number of other comments (far more than I have space to make) are also required.

First, I do not take the neutrality obligation to be likely to prevail under just any social conditions. Under conditions of tyranny, freedom and democracy might be restorable only if churches *do* support candidates for (public) office. A clear threat of such tyranny, as in pre-Nazi Germany, may also warrant such support. Nor do I take the obligation in question to be specifically religious or theological, since it need not be grounded in religious or theological elements and indeed not every religious tradition must contain elements that would sustain it. Whether the obligation has a sufficient moral basis depends in part on whether there are (as I think there may very well be) sufficient moral grounds for liberal democracy as the best form of government.[53] But even apart from how this question is resolved, there are considerations of good institutional citizenship and of prudence that support the principle of ecclesiastical political neutrality for churches living under conditions of freedom and democracy.

This neutrality principle will be too strong if we construe 'political' in the broad sense of 'contested in the arena of politics' or in the sense it has in 'political philosophy', wherein it means roughly 'concerning the appropriate or the basic structure of civil society' (a very wide notion is appropriate here encompassing both conceptual and normative notions). The term 'political' must be taken rather narrowly, so that moral issues are not included, even if they enter into distinctly political debates, but not so narrowly that pressing for restrictive laws or public policies[54]—such as policies requiring periods of prayer or meditation in public schools—does not count as political.

The difference between the political in the narrow sense and the moral can be masked by the application of a single term, such as 'the abortion issue', to both moral questions about its ethical permissibility and political questions about the degree of legal protection it should have. Paradigms of political questions are what specific people or what particular party will hold governmental power, what specific structure should be enacted for taxation, welfare, criminal justice, health care, and military systems, and what policies should govern relations, including immigration, with other countries. But there are many other political questions; some of these have major moral dimensions, and we cannot hope to make a plausible distinction between the moral and the political that is sharp enough to put every sociopolitical question clearly on one side or the other.

The separation of church and state does not require, nor do any sound principles demand, that churches should not publicly take moral positions, even if there is political controversy about them. Publicly taking moral positions is indeed a positive religious obligation in many religions. There are, to be sure, different ways of supporting moral positions. Some are closer than others to political statements, as where government officials of only one party are cited as immoral despite the prominence of comparable offenders who are officials in another party. These matters call for discretion and do not admit of codification.

In applying the ecclesiastical neutrality principle, it is important to distinguish—as with other politically significant institutions, such as universities—between *internal* and *external* political activities and, in both cases, between *official* and *unofficial* political statements and positions. The former activities are directed toward members, the latter toward an external group, such as society as a whole (these are the pure cases; there are myriad mixtures raising special problems that I cannot take up here). The principle of ecclesiastical political neutrality applies differently to the external than to the internal activities. A church's publicly promoting political candidates is, prima facie, poor institutional citizenship; its doing so internally need not be, though it may tend to corrupt the church's spiritual mission or may put undue pressure on its members, or both.[55]

It also matters considerably whether a church's political activity is official or unofficial, say carried on in private conversation as opposed to a letter to parishioners. Here again the internal-external distinction is relevant. Public support by clergy of a candidate for office may, especially when official, exert pressure on church members, on ordinary citizens, on candidates for public office (who may, e.g., curry favor or solicit opposing clerical statements), or on government officials (who may, for instance, think they are hearing, in the voice of one or more clergy, the wishes or views of the members of the relevant religious group).

The principle of ecclesiastical political neutrality would not undermine churches' encouraging their members' *participation* in politics; and it does not unduly restrict political participation by religious citizens, including clergy, or imply that they should not consider such participation an aspect of their religious commitments. A minister or rabbi could, under this principle, both publicly oppose nuclear dumping in the oceans and, during religious services, preach against political apathy. Civic indolence may be criticized both as a failing in a religious obligation to improve the world and as a moral vice in citizens. Taking political positions from the pulpit (and in other institutional ways), however, would be (prima facie) objectionable under the principle. Thus, a church-sponsored group, such as one opposing an unjust war, or a service committee that, in its humane activities, defies government policy, is not necessarily an official representative of the church's position. Even then, the group may distinguish its moral from its political aims, and prudence often dictates doing so.

To be sure, there are moral statements which, combined with certain obvious facts about politicians, government officials, or foreign powers, imply condemnation or approval of them. But there is a crucial difference between affirming moral truths which, *with* certain facts, imply political judgments, and, on the other hand, making political judgments themselves. Matters of fact may be controversial; and in any case, when the suggested distinction between the moral and the (narrowly) political is observed, the political bearing of factual issues is left to the individual judgment of those in the congregation or audience. That judgment constitutes an important filter between clerical deliverances and political action. Even people who accept the moral judgments in question, find it obvious how the facts are relevant, and draw an obviously implied political conclusion will have traversed a certain inferential distance. Doing so is an exercise of autonomy.[56]

I do *not* believe that the principle of ecclesiastical political neutrality should be written into law; but if it is not conscientiously observed, then candidates for public office may be unduly influenced to serve the special, even the distinctively religious, interests of certain churches, particularly if there is a majority church. Furthermore, the polarities afflicting relations between certain religious groups are more likely to surface in government decision making, where the public interest should be the overriding concern.

Admittedly, some polarization may arise from *any* public political disagreement, particularly when institutions themselves square off. But whereas in a free and democratic society, political controversy is inevitable, religious polarization is not. Moreover, some clergy represent themselves as having, or in any case are generally taken to have, special insight into matters of human conduct; this (among other factors) increases the chance of sociopolitical polarization if religious institutions as such enter into politics and (certain kinds of) public policy debate, even if they do it only or chiefly within their own congregations.

Granted, however hard we try to avoid basing political positions on religious considerations, there is no sharp distinction between moral and political issues, and certainly an admirable moral sermon on, for example, the duties of charity, could have obvious implications for legislative decisions on welfare policy. But if, in borderline cases, the moral and political intermingle, there is still a generally plain difference between, say, giving a moral sermon about the quality of contemporary movies and endorsing candidates, political parties, or politically contested public policy positions.

One might object to the ecclesiastical neutrality principle that the clergy are obligated to help bring into being a morally acceptable democracy and thus to promote, for example, economic justice, which might in turn require criticizing the government's policy on federal minimum wages.[57] Two distinctions are essential to appraising this objection. The first is between the clergy's obligations as citizens and their distinctively clerical obligations. The second is between the obligation to promote these ideals *in general*, especially as broadly moral, and the obligation to promote them *politically*, through specific parties or policies. I heartily acknowledge obligations of citizenship—and freedom of action—on the part of clergy. But I take it that argument is needed to show that the clergy *as such* are obligated to promote democracy, particularly if the promotion is to be political, e.g. by helping to elect a preferred party (among those committed to democracy in general); and I have argued that they are prima facie obligated not to promote candidates for office or specific laws or public policies that restrict human conduct. I agree that they should oppose, for instance, economic injustice; but proposing a specific wage structure or a detailed strategy of disarmament is quite another matter. Similarly, powerful opposition to racial injustice is to be expected of, for example, clergy in the Hebraic-Christian tradition, and it may be quite specific in terms of, say, real or imaginary examples of wrongdoing held up as abominable. But support of one political party's particular way of dealing with the problem, as opposed to a competing strategy proposed by another party, is quite different; that is (typically) one kind of thing the ecclesiastical neutrality principle is intended to restrict.

I believe it is—or should be—through the moral and spiritual power of churches that they improve society rather than through their direct exercises of political power; and I fear that churches' regularly exercising political power might produce religious fractures and quite possibly religious domination. Such domination, particularly in certain sectors of civic life, would wrongly limit the freedom of the religious and the non-religious alike. If there is a Protestant or Catholic or Jewish or Moslem position on a political issue, candidates may not only bend over backwards to win church endorsement on that issue, but also covet it in other areas. To some extent, this already occurs in the United States; and if there is, for instance, little enough disagreement, or ingenious enough compromise, or a wise enough clergy, or a sufficiently educated citizenry, democracy may still thrive. But it is more likely to thrive if the clergy judiciously abide by a reasonable standard of political neutrality.

The ecclesiastical principle of political neutrality must not be thought to be supported only by considerations of religious liberty and democratic ideals. It may also protect the integrity of religious institutions themselves. Politics and public policy are a complex and absorbing business, and to acquire the knowledge of them requisite to speak with the authority properly befitting a corporate church voice (or even an influential clerical voice) can easily reduce the time and commitment needed for spiritual and moral matters. It is one thing to criticize economic injustice in a general way; it is quite another to make a responsible judgment that the minimum wage should be raised or, say, increased to $5.55. The neutrality principle can thus help to prevent dilution of the clergy's religious function. As Moses gave the commandments of the Lord, the first is "You shall have no other Gods before me" (20 Exodus 3, and 5 Deuteronomy 7); and Jesus taught that one cannot serve God and mammon (7 Matthew 24). Politics should be a worthier pursuit than money and other false gods, but we must still ask how well one can serve God and the state.

There are external as well as internal factors that support the ecclesiastical neutrality principle. For one thing, political action by churches exposes them to retaliation of a kind that they might be able to avoid. One might argue, for instance, that without a significant degree of political neutrality, churches would at best have had more difficulty than they in fact did in surviving under communism in Europe. It might also be argued that their moral and spiritual force had more to do with bringing repressive regimes down than any specifically political agenda or activity that they engaged in or might have undertaken.

Clerical neutrality

At this point I want to reiterate that the ecclesiastical neutrality principle is institutional; it does not imply that clergy should not take personal and even public positions on topics connected with politics or public policy, or even concerning personalities in government. To be sure, in some churches, what the clergy say even privately might be taken for church doctrine; but there is still a great difference between what is so interpreted and what is publicly announced as church doctrine or policy, or paid out from church coffers. Even in making avowedly personal statements or in giving private counsel, however, clergy who believe in freedom and democracy should follow an individual *principle of clerical political neutrality* to the effect that clergy (as individuals) have a prima facie obligation to (1) observe a distinction, especially in making public statements, between their personal political views and those of their office or otherwise held by them *as* clergy, (2) prevent any political aims that they may have from dominating their professional conduct as clergy, and (3) abstain from officially (as religious leaders) supporting candidates for public office or pressing for laws or policies that would restrict human conduct. Domination by political aims is possible even where (e.g. in a sermon) one specifies that one is not speaking for one's church institutionally; disclaimers of that kind, however, can help in keeping official statements distinct from expressions of personal conviction.

This principle is quite consistent both with the point that applying religious principles and insights to issues of law and public policy can be highly beneficial and with the clergy as individuals following the rationale and motivation principles—with all the freedom to use religious reasons that this implies. The judicious application of religious principles and insights may have heuristic value in leading to the discovery of new points. It may serve as a moral corrective, for instance in exposing injustices, whether against religious groups or anyone else. It may strengthen moral motivation, especially by bringing religious commitments together with secular moral considerations in the service of sound social policies. It may reduce strife and recrimination among disparate social groups, as where tolerance and forgiveness are stressed as part of a religious commitment or mediation among religious denominations is accomplished by judiciously stressing what they have in common. It may enhance the aesthetic and cultural aspects of civic life, in part by uniting religious ideals and traditions central in a culture with sociopolitical standards acceptable to both the religious and the non-religious alike. And it may encourage a vivid and salutary modeling of the forms of life that people cherish as part of their religious faith, as where charity and community service are avowedly given as an expression of religious ideals.

As substantial as the benefits of applying religious insights and principles to public policy issues are, it is appropriate that clergy exercise restraint—*clerical virtue*, we might say—in touching on political issues, even in unofficial conduct and particularly in public. If they do not, they invite peers who disagree to use religious leverage for opposite ends; and the public, quite possibly including their own congregations, may suffer. There is certainly a risk of inducing political discord in congregations that might otherwise enjoy a deeper unity. There is also the danger of polarizing a congregation by bringing to the fore divisive political issues that could be appropriately dealt with in a different setting.

Departures from the principle of clerical political neutrality also raise, in addition to the danger of dilution of clerical function, the risk of influencing one's congregation toward placing political aims over spiritual and non-political moral ones, such as those concerning relations with family and friends. It easily seems more important to put others' houses in order than one's own; and even to the righteous, the latter task, typically involving so many more people, can seem much more important.

This is a good place to record a keen awareness that in fact much of the impetus for many major reforms in human history—including, to a significant degree, liberalism as a political philosophy—has come, and continues to come, from religious inspiration or commitment. There are some reflective people who believe that if the religious contribution to this impetus is reduced, there will not be sufficient unselfish motivation to enable contemporary civilization to overcome its problems. I do not know to what extent this last point holds, but it should be plain that I am not proposing to reduce the reformative influence of religious inspiration and commitment. My hope is that it will be constrained only where necessary for sound ideals sharable among at least many religious people and that it will be united with secular motivation toward the same desirable ends.

Some Problems of Application

Application of the principles of secular rationale, secular motivation, theo-ethical equilibrium, and ecclesiastical and clerical neutrality can be complicated because there may be considerable

difficulty in determining whether a reason one has for doing or believing something is secular, or constitutes an evidentially adequate
ground, as well as in deciding whether it is fact motivating. These
difficulties merit extensive study. Here I simply offer three suggestions. First, we should be guided by what we can learn from considering paradigms of both kinds of reason, evidential and motivational:
there is much to be learned from asking, of what seem our most
cogent reasons, why they justify, and, of our most moving reasons,
why they influence us. Second, wherever the two kinds of reason
(evidential and motivating) diverge on a major issue, we should in-
quire why.

The third suggestion requires one to seek outside help. In borderline cases where the secular status of a reason is in question we
should consider whether it would be taken to be secular by a reflective person who sincerely and comprehendingly claims to be non-
religious and considers it carefully.[58] A religious consideration,
viewed from inside a religious tradition to which it belongs, need
have no theological identifying marks and easily seems to be second
nature (or perhaps a dictate of purely natural law); but from the
outside, such an element can often be seen to be rooted in a tradition
the outsider recognizes as religious and may find alienating.

The difficulty of determining whether a reason one has is a
motivating element in one's sociopolitical conduct is especially
likely to occur long before the relevant action or long afterwards.
But what the motivation principle (beyond the rationale principle)
requires of conscientious citizens contemplating support of restrictive laws or policies is at most three manageable efforts. First, they
should try to formulate all the significant reasons they have for each
major option—itself often a very useful exercise. Second, where one
or more reasons is religious, they should consider the motivational
weight of each reason taken by itself as well as in the context of the
others (if none is religious, the principle does not imply any need to
go any further into motivation, though some other principle may).
Third, they should attempt to ascertain, by considering hypothetical
situations and felt motivational or cognitive impulses or tendencies,
whether each reason is motivationally sufficient. We should ask ourselves, for example, what really impresses us as supporting the proposition; what occurs to us first (or most spontaneously) on the

matter; whether we would believe something if we did not accept a certain premise for it; and whether a given reason taken by itself seems persuasive to us, in the sense of providing a sense of surety. We should also listen carefully to our own voices. If we are adhering to the principle of secular motivation, and if we would speak with a truly civic voice, at least one secular reason should emerge as suitably motivating us.

In short, my two main first-order principles of civic virtue imply that one should ask of one's reasons certain evidential, historical, and hypothetical questions. Adhering to the (second-order) principle of theo-ethical equilibrium can often help in this task, as well as in applying the principles of ecclesiastical and clerical neutrality. One must, with all three of these principles, use practical wisdom in deciding how much effort to expend in a given case of contemplated action.

Practical wisdom is also crucial in determining how much of one's public discourse should be couched in religious terms. Even if one is scrupulously abiding by the secular motivation principle, one may still have and present religious reasons for one's sociopolitical views. The principles of secular rationale and secular motivation concern advocacy and support of a certain range of laws and public policies; they do not restrict freedom of speech or preclude the use of religious reasons in many other ways. Nor do they imply that religion should be "privatized," as if it were something that had to be kept to oneself, or that it should be marginal in influencing public life.[59]

The rationale and motivation principles do not even imply that one need necessarily hesitate to appeal publicly to religious reasons in support of a widely contested view if it is purely moral, as where abortion is said to be morally wrong because it destroys a gift of God. Neither the crucial premise for this moral conclusion nor the conclusion itself entails that abortion should be illegal in a free and democratic society, and stating the premise, even publicly, does not automatically count as supporting a coercive law or public policy. There are, moreover, ways to offer the argument even in public policy contexts (e.g., by taking care to bring these limitations out) that do not imply one's supporting restrictive laws or public policies.[60]

One may, however, easily be wrong in thinking that bringing religious reasons to bear on a moral question or, especially, a public policy issue, will make one more convincing; one may instead polarize the discussion. It can well turn out that advancing religious reasons for a controversial social policy leads the opposition to advance conflicting religious reasons. This, in turn, can lead to suspicions about the motivation or the cogency of even the secular reasons on each side; and while people who seek theo-ethical equilibrium may often be prepared to revise their secular as well as their religious views, this disposition is not always present, and deadlock may occur where compromise would have been possible.

Fortunately, if the motivation principle is widely accepted by the parties to a dispute—indeed, perhaps even if it is not—and if one is in good communication with people who disagree on the issue at hand, one will likely get substantial help from them in determining what one's motivating reasons in the dispute are. Whenever religious reasons seem to them motivationally too strong, people who disagree on the issue in question should be expected to help one probe one's grounds. Others hear our voice better than we do. They may also think of revealing questions about us that we ourselves overlook, or observe words or deeds that teach us something we did not realize about our own thinking or motivation.[61]

It could be that most people are not usually good at forming reasonable judgments regarding even what reasons they have, much less which of these reasons, if any, are motivating.[62] If this is so, the effort to find out may be all the more needed: if, through self-examination, I cannot tell what my reasons for a belief or desire of mine are, I should probably wonder whether I have any normatively adequate reasons for it; and I am likely to make better decisions if I try to find some good reasons for the relevant belief or desires. If, moreover, I cannot tell pretty accurately which reasons motivate me and about how much they do so at least relative to other reasons, I cannot adequately understand myself or reasonably predict my own behavior.

Given the self-examination that, for some people, may be required for conscientious adherence to the rationale and motivation principles, it may appear that some religious people would be excluded from "full participation in political debate and action on some important issues."[63] To assess this, we must distinguish the two quite different cases of debate and (other) action, such as voting for more restrictive abortion laws. We should also distinguish *full* participation in debate from *unrestricted* participation. I can participate fully in political debate—even dominantly—whether or not I use all my arguments or express all my sentiments. To be sure, if I have only religious considerations to bring to a debate—something that, given the case for the possibility of theo-ethical equilibrium, seems unlikely to hold for informed, reflective people on important matters—then the rationale principle may lead me not to use them in certain ways. I may, for instance, point out their bearing but may not advocate coercive legislation on the basis of them. That, however, is a restraint I would wish to be observed by people who, for *their* religious reasons, want to restrict my liberty.

As to the case of action, *any* moral principle applying to sociopolitical conduct will restrict it in some cases. But I can adhere to the rationale and motivation principles and still fully participate in political action even concerning abortion and even aimed at producing its rejection: I can prominently and forcefully support policies, candidates, and parties that seek to *dissuade* people from doing it. What I may not do without adequate secular reason (unless my obligation under the secular rationale principle is overridden) is advocate or support *coercive* laws or public policies on this or other matters that concern me. That, too, is a kind of restraint I would wish to be observed by members of other religious groups who would want to coerce my behavior in the direction of their religiously preferred standards.

This is a good place to emphasize four points about the rationale and motivation principles. Together these points help to show what my principles do not exclude and how large a role they accommodate for religious considerations in the political arena.

First, they are each independent of the principle of theo-ethical equilibrium and so do not require bearing any additional burden it may impose. But although they do not entail that principle, it is helpful in applying them. Moreover, neither the rationale principle nor the motivation principle is presupposed by the equilibrium principle itself or by the broad view that civic virtue requires (for religious people) seeking theo-ethical equilibrium; I simply present them as good candidates for a role in realizing civic virtue.

Second, the principle of secular motivation allows that one may *also* have religious reasons and be motivated by them. One may indeed believe them more basic than the secular reasons that motivate one in sociopolitical matters, as in the case of someone who thinks that the most basic reasons for a principle, though not the only adequate reasons for it, are religious (here one might again think of the Ten Commandments). The ideal for religious citizens is a special kind of cooperation between the religious and the secular, not the domination of the former by the latter. That cooperation requires that some secular reason play a minimal role, but not that the person *regard* that role as primary or *take* the secular to be more important than the religious or even independent of it.

Third, my use of such separationist principles by no means presupposes that religious reasons cannot be evidentially adequate. My principles also allow that religious reasons may be motivationally *sufficient* for a political stance (though not motivationally necessary, since secular reasons could not then be motivationally sufficient— they would be unable to produce belief or action without the cooperation of religious elements).

Fourth, my principles allow that religious reasons can be *causally sufficient* for producing a secular justification of a law or public policy, in the sense that one's having such reasons can, say through one's thinking about them or about related considerations, lead one to discover an evidentially adequate secular reason. That reason in turn can be motivationally sufficient (even independently of its continuing to receive support from the religious factors leading to its discovery). In the orders of discovery and motivation, either religious or secular reasons can be primary, and both can cooperate evidentially or motivationally.

The rationale and motivation principles even allow a virtuous citizen's judging the religious reasons in question to be more important than the secular ones, or being more *strongly* motivated by them, or both; this is perfectly consistent with one's being sufficiently motivated by adequate secular reason. Holding such judgments is also compatible with adhering to the clerical principle of political neutrality. The principles simply aim at preventing a certain kind of domination by religious reasons in contexts in which they should be constrained, and adhering to the principles makes it much easier to speak with an appropriate civic voice.

To be sure, in public advocacy of laws and policies that restrict human conduct, it seems *generally* best to conduct discussion in secular terms; but there may be special contexts in which candor or other considerations require laying out all of one's main reasons.[64] If one does articulate religious reasons in a public debate, it should help to be able to express both commitment to the principle of secular rationale and reasons that accord with it. This would show a respect for a religiously neutral point of view that any rational citizen may share.[65] The principles of secular rationale and motivation may, however, be adhered to without being stated or even consciously endorsed and may be minimally satisfied even by those who have never heard of them or would reject them. It is the reasons one has and is motivated by that matter most, not what one would say about one's reasons or about the principles those reasons should satisfy.

Although the rationale and motivation principles (and indeed everything I have contended here) are entirely consistent with religious reasons' being evidentially adequate, the evidential adequacy of those reasons is not a presupposition of liberal democracy—nor, of course, is their evidential inadequacy.[66] Indeed, it may be that the absence of both presuppositions is a negative commitment of liberal democracy, a special kind of neutrality regarding religious matters, one that seems to go somewhat beyond neutrality toward religious institutions. It would be inappropriate for a liberal theory to contain either epistemological claim, just as it would violate the neutrality of a liberal state toward religion to support anti-religious practices or institutions as such.[67] This epistemological neutrality perhaps need not be a positive plank in even a fully articulated democratic constitution, but it is an important strand in much liberal democratic theory.

Religious commitment is not, in its mature embodiments, a monolithic position of blind obedience but a complex, multi-layered fidelity to a multifarious array of texts, traditions, authoritative directives, religious experiences, and people in and outside one's own religious community. A mature religious commitment may require sensitivity, reflection, self-renewal, and, often, the practical wisdom to reconcile conflicting elements. Any educated religious person, however, who comes to the obligations of citizenship in a liberal democracy is already aware of plural bases, both religious and secular, of moral and sociopolitical obligation, and of the fallibility of even one's careful interpretations of those sources and obligations. The cultivation of civic virtue should reflect this sense of multiplicity and tension. That same sense helps in seeing the need for institutional separation of church and state, with each keeping an appropriate distance from the other and concentrating on its proper function.

Neither the institutional separation of church and state that I have defended nor any reasonable separation of the religious and the political in the conduct of individuals need retard the forces of progress, whether they are inspired religiously or morally or in both ways, nor should my proposed principles force anyone adhering to them to make religion a purely private matter or marginalize it in life as a whole. In the service of religious ideals, as in realizing secular moral standards, injustice in all its forms may be fought. Corruption and dishonesty may be rooted out. The ignorant may be taught. The practice of the arts and humanities, and of religion and the sciences, may be promoted among all peoples. The sick may be given comfort, the poor relief, the lonely fellowship.

In religious traditions that recognize God as omniscient, omnipotent, and omnibenevolent, there is good reason to expect that one can, by and large, achieve an equilibrium between religious and secular considerations in relation to major moral and sociopolitical principles crucial for guiding civic life in a free society. Seeking that equilibrium is in any case a worthy goal, both for individuals and for institutions, particularly churches. That quest can contribute both to understanding each set of sources of obligation and to one's justification for affirming the obligations in question. Far from reducing one's inclination to be a politically active citizen, it can add to one's motivation to fulfill one's civic obligations. It can also enhance communication with others in different traditions. Both in achieving such equilibrium, and in our efforts to exhibit civic virtue, the principles of secular rationale and secular motivation, and the related ecclesiastical and clerical neutrality principles, are among the reasonable guides we may follow. They can also help in cultivating and in using an appropriate civic voice. To achieve such equilibrium, and to realize civic virtue, is to contribute to the liberty, mutual respect, and cooperative exchange of ideas that best nourishes both religious practice and moral conduct. Perhaps it is also part of the civic realization of the injunction of beneficence: the injunction to love one's neighbor as oneself.[68]

Notes

1. This is worded to leave open whether a liberal state might permissibly promote religion as such, a question treated below.

2. In describing and supporting these three principles I draw on—and greatly abbreviate—a section of my "The Separation of Church and State and the Obligations of Citizens," *Philosophy & Public Affairs* 18, no. 3 (1989): pp. 259–96.

3. A liberal democracy need not protect, in the name of religious freedom, practices that violate basic human rights, as where people are burned to death in sacrifice. But there is no easy way to determine the range of these rights nor the appropriate sanctions for the state to impose should they be violated. The principles defended below are intended to constitute part of a framework of decision, but they are not by themselves sufficient for the task.

4. This restriction does not rule out teaching children moral principles that are commonly part of one or more religious traditions—a point that is not always appreciated, sometimes with the unfortunate effect that schoolteachers are reluctant to teach moral principles.

5. These features are stressed by William P. Alston in *Philosophy of Language* (Englewood Cliffs, NJ: Prentice-Hall, 1964), p. 88 (I have abbreviated and slightly revised his list). This characterization does not entail that a religion must be theistic, but theistic religions are my main concern (even in non-theistic religions, the relevant moral code tends to be given a somewhat similar privileged status in relation to appropriate items on this list, such as the world view, the sacred and profane, and certain rituals, such as marriage). It is noteworthy that in *United States v Seeger*, 380 US 163 (1965) the Supreme Court ruled that religious belief need not be theistic; but, for reasons that will become increasingly apparent below, theistic religions raise the most important church-state issues at least for societies like those in the Western world. For discussion of the significance of *Seeger* in relation to church-state aspects of the foundations of liberalism see Abner S. Greene, "Uncommon Ground," a review essay on John Rawls's *Political Liberalism* (New York: Columbia University Press, 1993) and Ronald Dworkin's *Life's Dominion* in *George Washington Law Review* 62, no. 4 (1994): pp. 646–673.

6. Conscientious objector status is debatable: is allowing it only for religious reasons inadmissible preferential treatment, or is it required in recognition of religious freedom? Even if the latter holds, it is arguable that freedom of religion is being unwarrantedly preferred over freedom of secular conscience. For discussion

of the nature of governmental neutrality and a case for it as essential in a liberal democracy see Charles Larmore, *Patterns of Moral Complexity* (Cambridge and New York: Cambridge University Press, 1987), especially chap. 3. A different case for governmental neutrality, with a partial account of the liberal basis of impartiality toward religion, is given by Thomas Nagel in "Moral Conflict and Political Legitimacy," *Philosophy & Public Affairs* 16, no. 3 (1987): pp. 215–40.

7. On the constitutionality of public institutions' having or requiring the Pledge, with discussion of the church-state implications of the issue, see Abner S. Greene, "The Pledge of Allegiance Problem," *Fordham Law Review* 64, no. 2 (1995): pp. 451–90.

8. The language of this sentence will remind some readers of the much-discussed "Lemon test" for the propriety of legislation: "First, the statute must have a secular legislative purpose; second, its principal or primary effect must be one that neither advances nor inhibits religion; finally, the statute must not foster 'an excessive entanglement with religion'." See *Lemon v Kurtzmann* 403 US 602 (1971). Apart from the point that it is obvious that "excessive" entanglement should be avoided, the first two clauses are deservedly controversial. This essay addresses some of the relevant issues, such as a possible voucher system for public education, in less vague terms (though some degree of vagueness is inevitable on such matters).

9. Calling the kinds of obligations in question *religious* is not meant to presuppose the truth of theism. If it is objected that apart from God's existence there are no religious obligations (at least for those who take them to be ordained by God), we could simply speak of *presumptively religious* obligations, referring to the kind reasonably taken to be incumbent on votaries of a particular religion as such, and proceed: the kinds of church-state issues under discussion would be largely unaffected.

10. Perhaps those with resources giving everything they have to the poor is an example pertinent in this context, though the force of Jesus' directive is open to more than one interpretation.

11. This formulation applies both to *types* of conduct (the more problematic case) and their *tokenings*, the specific performances of those types by an agent at a time. A particular person's obligation to A—say to give money to a particular church-supported cause—could, at a specific moment, be grounded in secular considerations, such as the effectiveness of its famine relief work, even if the primary grounds of *the* obligation to A (for virtually all who have it) are religious. Then, the specific act token—donating a sum in writing a particular check—might be at least in part secularly grounded even though the same person might have written a similar check a week earlier entirely for a religious reason. Deeds of the same action type, such as donations to a church or synagogue, may be performed (tokened) at different times for different reasons, or different combinations of reasons, among the reasons there are for deeds of that type. When agent, time, and circumstance are fixed, there may, for a token of a religiously obligatory deed, be only a secular reason or only a religious reason or a happy marriage of the two.

12. Such an entailment may hold for some propositions, but apparently not for *every* proposition supported by a source. This is by no means beyond controversy; certainly scripture, religious authority, and tradition tend to overlap in regard to the obligations they imply are incumbent on believers. But my purposes here do not require that there be no exceptions to the independence claim.

13. Jesus says, e.g., that the greatest commandments are to love one's God with all one's heart and to love one's neighbor as oneself; and given the way in which the Ten Commandments are ordered and expressed by Moses, together with their role in the Hebrew Bible in general, there is some reason to think the order of their presentation may indicate a kind of relative importance.

14. It is useful to compare John Rawls's notion of public reason in this context. The notion seems narrower than that of a secular reason, but usable for some of the same purposes. See his *Political Liberalism*. Some of my case for constraints on the use of religious reasons applies also to certain secular reasons, especially those that cannot play a proper role in public policy debate in a liberal democracy. Some of the latter, e.g. certain esoteric reasons, would be construed as inappropriate for that role by my requirement of (justificatory) adequacy, but I cannot go into this matter here.

15. The notion of fallibilism here may raise the question of the appropriate attitude for those who believe in papal infallibility. It should be noted that this doctrine is restricted both as to content, covering above all moral matters, and as to manner of expression: it applies only to pronouncements *ex cathedra*. Since there can be vagueness on both counts, a measure of fallibilism may be appropriate concerning any *interpretation* of what is regarded as infallible in content. My concern here is also with quite specific sociopolitical matters; and on these even people who give authority an enormous role in their lives may wish to be fallibilistic regarding their own judgments of what they should do *as citizens*.

16. A weaker condition would require only the capacity to understand the grounds, but I doubt that this condition would be sufficiently strong. Actual identification, however, is not required; since we are not talking about ideally rational citizens, such things as confusion or prejudice can interfere.

17. This is a partial reply to Michael J. Perry's contention against John Rawls and me (and implicitly against the liberal tradition in political philosophy as expressed in, e.g., John Stuart Mill's *On Liberty*) that it is not clear why we fail to show the respect owed people as free and equal citizens when we offer them, in explaining a coercive law, what we take to be our best reasons for it (so long as we do not imply their inferior humanity). See *Religion in Politics: Constitutional and Moral Perspectives* (forthcoming from Oxford University Press) (chap. 2). My suggestion is that even one's best reasons can be unsound or partisan or even bigoted. Cf. T. M. Scanlon's contractarian approach to understanding this issue in "Contractarianism and Utilitarianism," in *Utilitarianism and Beyond*, eds. Amartya Sen and Bernard Williams (Cambridge: Cambridge University Press, 1982).

18. I use 'standard Western theism' with some hesitation. The idea may be in part a philosophers' construction, but there is a recognizable set of assumptions here. What follows will clarify the idea, which was introduced for a similar purpose in my "The Place of Religious Argument in a Free and Democratic Society," *San Diego Law Review* 30, no. 4 (1993): pp. 677–702.

19. It would not be unqualifiedly impossible, since one might be moral from good fortune as opposed to being so as an application of one's moral knowledge. I assume, what all but a few radical theists grant, that even if rejection of God can be a moral wrong, it is not the only kind of moral wrong, nor does it make all the others insignificant.

20. It should be granted that a non-religious route to religious truths could con-

ceivably lead through them, e.g. through divine commands, to moral truths; but this pathway to moral truths, however impeccable logically, still runs through religious territory, and some rational citizens in a liberal democracy might be permissibly unwilling to follow it as an essential path to those moral truths, say as their only way of grasping why they must give up a liberty. For some, it might be religiously inappropriate to be so led by someone else; for others it might be objectionable to be led through religious premises at all.

21. If natural properties include theological ones, e.g. being commanded by God, then the case for the existence of secular grounds for moral truths becomes more problematic. But the relevant properties of God (as opposed to, say, power) are not usually considered natural. Moreover, if they are natural, it may be that moral properties could supervene on them *by virtue of* supervening more basically on other, "earthly" natural ones: God might, e.g., command honesty because of what it is to be honest as opposed to deceitful, i.e., because of the (ontically) constitutive natural properties of honesty. Thus the obligatoriness of honesty would supervene directly on its divine requiredness, which would in turn supervene on its appropriateness to relations among persons. Call this the *embeddedness* of natural base properties in theological properties (it can take various forms, which I cannot distinguish here). Alternatively, one might say simply that God commands honesty because it is necessarily right (or good or both). On this view, God infallibly sees the rightness of honesty through comprehending its natural basis, as opposed to determining that basis by sheer will, in a sense implying that, e.g., lying and murder could have been right. This line of thought may be the more plausible conception of divine moral commands and would be consistent with honesty's supervening on natural properties apart from embeddedness.

22. What does commonly happen is that we cannot be sure what our obligations *on balance* are even when we know, from natural facts, what our prima facie obligations are. The secularly based moral map is thus limited—a point crucial for Kent Greenawalt, who argues that (as I would put it) where there is an appropriate kind of secular indeterminacy on certain moral issues individuals may properly rely, even in the political domain, on religions considerations to decide their conduct, including voting. See *Religious Convictions and Political Choice* (Oxford and New York: Oxford University Press, 1988). I would stress that there may be similar problems in the religious domain, e.g. where two prima facie commandments in the Decalogue conflict. For critical discussion of Greenawalt's view in this book see my "Religion and the Ethics of Political Participation," *Ethics* 100, no. 2 (1990): pp. 386–97.

23. This is cautiously worded in part because it cannot be assumed without argument that religious (or moral) obligations outweigh all others; hence, it cannot simply be assumed that God must wish us, on balance, to prefer realizing a religious obligation over a moral one where the two conflict. The case of Abraham and Isaac of course comes to mind. Note, however, that even if we knew that God placed (one or more) religious obligations over moral ones, we could still have better reason for believing that God commands, say, protection of one's children than to believe that God commands any particular action inconsistent with this. Should Abraham, however, *insofar as he (reasonably?) believed that it was God requiring the sacrifice*, have believed that sacrificing his son was inconsistent with protecting him? That is not clear: God's ways of protecting us are infinite. Note, too, how the story ends: the morally forbidden action is not required after all, perhaps suggesting that

despite appearances, there cannot be an inconsistency between religious and moral obligation. This, however, would be false comfort for Kantians and certain other moral theorists: Abraham has already done the immoral deed at the level of willing—and "in his own heart."

24. Cf. Lenn Goodman's view that "for monotheism goodness is constitutive in the idea of God" and that "Ethics is constitutive in framing our idea of God but does not exhaust its content, and theism is a source of moral resolve and sublimity of principle but far from being the sole source at which such values can be tapped. All human beings know a good deal about their obligations without turning to God." See *God of Abraham* (Oxford and New York: Oxford University Press, 1996), pp. 81, 83.

25. Depending on one's theology, this might apply to a secular ground for which there is no religious counterpart ground that supports the same normative conclusion, as well as to a religious ground that seems isolated from supporting secular considerations. On common theistic assumptions, however, if there is a cogent truth-entailing secular reason for a normative conclusion, then God believes that conclusion (like any other truth), and the absence of any specifically theological ground should not prevent one's acting on the conclusion. Note, too, that disequilibrium between theistic and secular elements is a stronger reason for reluctance than is mere lack of integration; my suggestion, however, is that a positive integration should, in major moral matters, be expected to be achievable. If, for instance, those who think on religious grounds (and perhaps other grounds) that abortion in the first trimester is killing a person cannot convince conscientious people whose morality they otherwise fully respect to accept the point, they should consider this a datum in disequilibrium with their theo-ethical view.

26. Stephen L. Carter criticizes Kent Greenawalt, Bruce Ackerman, John Rawls, and me on this score, suggesting that "religious citizens are forced to split off vital components of their personalities." See *The Culture of Disbelief* (New York: Anchor Books, 1994), p. 230. Here I reply from my point of view, but some of what I say might apply to the other positions, especially Greenawalt's in, e.g., *Private Consciences and Public Reasons* (New York and Oxford: Oxford University Press, 1995), especially chaps. 2–8.

27. A possible example is Timothy P. Jackson's agapistic liberalism (as I would call it). Holding that Christianity puts charity first as a reason for action, he says, "The Christian is enjoined to 'make love *your* aim' (1 Corinthians 14:1), not merely to make love *an* aim . . ." See "Love in a Liberal Society: A Response to Paul J. Weithman," *Journal of Religious Ethics* 22, no. 1 (1994): pp. 29–38.

28. In "Acting from Virtue," *Mind* 104, no. 414 (1995): pp. 449–71, I discuss how virtues and principles interact in a virtuous agent and what it is to act from virtue. So far as principles in relation to virtue ethics are concerned, it is noteworthy that Aristotle himself says that there are some actions, such as murder, adultery, and theft, that do not admit of a mean, with the clear implication that they are "as a rule" wrong. See *Nicomachean Ethics* 1107a10ff. For an account of Aristotle bearing on this point and arguing that Aristotle took himself to be able to establish theoretically significant ethical generalizations, see T. E. Irwin, "Ethics as An Inexact Science," forthcoming.

29. See "The Separation of Church and State and the Obligations of Citizenship," cited above. The principle applies with different degrees of force in different

contexts. Moreover, the adequacy requirement rules out some *non*-religious reasons, e.g. those that are ill-grounded; but my concern here is with the specifically religious in relation to the political. I might add that the principle is not meant to require that an adequate reason be objectively correct in a sense implying that it is equivalent to a true proposition. A false proposition that is sufficiently well justified can count as an adequate reason. My paper just cited spoke of an adequate reason for something as one "whose truth is sufficient to justify" that, and at least one careful commentator on the paper has read this conjunctively rather than conditionally; i.e., as implying both truth and justificatory sufficiency, rather than (as intended) on the model of, e.g., 'You need a witness whose testimony for your side is sufficient to sway those in doubt', which does not imply that either the witness or the testimony is actual. An alternative wording is 'a reason which, if it should be true, justifies . . .'. See Philip L. Quinn, "Political Liberalisms and Their Exclusions of the Religious," *Proceedings and Addresses of the American Philosophical Association* 69, no. 2 (1995): pp. 35–56, especially 38–39.

30. It does not, e.g., imply the possibility of existing apart from divine creation. In case it should seem that affirming the evidential independence of God on the part of reasons is somehow irreverent, let me note that the most famous arguments for the existence of God are supposed to have premises with just this status: if they did not, they would fail of their purpose, which is roughly to provide evidential ground for believing God exists, on the basis of considerations not dependent on one's already having that ground.

31. Moral skepticism is not easily refuted, but I have attacked some of its most plausible forms in "Skepticism in Theory and Practice: Justification and Truth, Rationality and Goodness," chap. 3 of my *Moral Knowledge and Ethical Character*, forthcoming from Oxford University Press, 1997. A positive non-skeptical moral epistemology is developed in chaps. 2, 4, 5, and 11.

32. Perhaps the most influential treatment of prima facie reasons is that of W. D. Ross in *The Right and the Good* (Oxford: Oxford University Press, 1930). I discuss Ross's conception in detail, clarify it, and bring out how knowledge of major moral principles can have a basis in secular reason in "Intuitionism, Pluralism, and the Foundations of Ethics," in *Moral Knowledge?*, eds. Walter Sinnott-Armstrong and Mark Timmons (Oxford and New York; Oxford University Press, 1996).

33. See Kent Greenawalt's *Private Consciences and Public Reasons*, p. 67.

34. "The Separation of Church and State," especially pp. 284–86.

35. It has been claimed otherwise, e.g., by Vern Sima, in a letter to the *Lincoln Journal-Star* (23 October 1993): "I belong to a church that teaches abortion is murder. I am open-minded enough to accept the church's unbounded wisdom. But what ultimately convinced me was scientific evidence and observation. What we have here is science confirming religious truths, not religious truths standing alone, even though that would be enough." This claim is not plausible to me because, for one thing, I cannot see why one must be open-minded to accept what one conceives as "unbounded wisdom" or why, if one thinks that the church's view manifests it, one would not be convinced *before* discovering the scientific evidence. The question is especially urgent given that the writer says the religious truth "would be enough," apparently meaning that the church's view would not *need* scientific confirmation to be acceptable. Detailed treatment of what constitutes religious argumentation is provided in my "The Place of Religious Argument in a Free and Democratic Society," cited above.

Compare the claim that "There is no longer any serious scientific dispute that the unborn child is a human creature who dies violently in the act of abortion. This brute fact is the root of our national distress over the abortion license." See "The America We Seek: A Statement of Pro-Life Principle and Concern," signed by Michael Novak and Ralph Reed among dozens of others, *First Things* 63 (May 1996): p. 40. This statement treats the claim following "dispute" as scientific. But if being a child entails, as it ordinarily does, being a person, or if being a creature entails being created by God, then the claim is apparently not scientific but theological or philosophical or both. If, on the other hand, a creature is just a living thing, and a child is a genetically human entity in *any* stage of development from that of zygote on, then the supposed brute fact does not appear to sustain the anti-abortion conclusions it is used to support. We might ponder the question whether so many conscientious people would let this kind of ambiguity go unremarked apart from religious motivation to establish their conclusion regarding abortion. And might the attempt to establish that conclusion scientifically bespeak a sense that a secular rationale is needed for justified coercion and perhaps that secular motivation is needed for the conscientious imposition of that coercion?

36. Not just any anti-religious motivation would fail to count as secular, e.g. where the desire is simply to weaken a religious group enough to prevent its dominating a society. But for purposes of taking the motivation principle to be an element in civic virtue it is reasonable to construe a desire to destroy a religion or to discredit its deity as non-secular.

37. The accrediting may take account of certain factors that are not purely academic. It is one thing to give vouchers to support free parental choice, including religious choice; it is another to allow them where racial discrimination is practiced. It is a delicate and difficult question when criteria of admission are objectionable in a way that warrants differential governmental treatment.

38. It is noteworthy that in The Netherlands the government funds both public and sectarian schools, compensating, in part, for the differences this allows among publicly funded schools by requiring national examinations keyed to a core curriculum constituting eighty per cent of what students study in the secondary school years. For a brief description see the article by Laurel Shaper Walters in the *Christian Science Monitor*, 12 December 1992.

39. One may wonder how a religious person who seeks to do everything in fulfillment of God's will can abide by the principle of secular motivation. Recall the earlier point that such a person can without irreverence be motivated by the sense of just conduct as dictated by the dignity of persons, at least where being thus dictated is equivalent to the property of being commanded by God. The same point surely holds where the person justifiedly *believes* this equivalence to hold (and perhaps even in certain cases in which the belief is not justified). Even if, in addition, such a person is not sufficiently motivated by any secular consideration *without* thinking of it as religiously acceptable, on a liberal reading of the principle of secular motivation—more liberal than I gave it in "The Separation of Church and State"— the person can still be sufficiently motivated by that consideration. If the person is motivated by the consideration and not just by the thought that God commands the action it supports, this would be a case of being motivated *by a secular consideration*, without being (purely) *secularly motivated*. It would not be a pure instance of *civic* virtue, since the motivation in question depends on the belief that the consider-

ation in question is religiously acceptable, but this consideration would at least not be a mere rationalization and would, in addition, be a candidate to satisfy the principle of secular rationale. I am not here endorsing the suggested liberal reading of the principle of secular motivation, but it is important to see that as stated the principle can bear that reading.

40. Accessibility in the relevant sense is no simple matter: ordinary sensory data of the kind needed to use a ruler and read a gauge are clearly accessible, and a clairvoyant sense about the future is clearly not. But it might be argued that anyone who is open-minded, considers natural theology, and attends certain religious services in a good-faith effort to find God thereby has access to good theistic reasons for a certain view of the world. Many people who reluctantly or ambivalently leave their faith would claim to be counterexamples to this; but even if that judgment is accepted, the notion of accessibility is not precise and will remain controversial.

41. This does not imply that these propositions are necessarily true simpliciter, but that it is impossible that they be *both* endorsed or accepted by God and false. Thus, one may presumably be as certain of their truth as one is that they are divinely endorsed or accepted. For many people this is a very high degree of certainty.

42. Stephen Carter puts a related point vividly when he says, "I have always been deeply offended by politicians, whether on the left or on the right, who are ready to seize on the language and symbols of religion in order to grub for votes" (op. cit., p. 47).

43. It is worth noting two points here. (1) Nothing I have said about religious reasons entails that religion is necessarily either "esoteric" or in any way irrational, or even that there cannot be cogent arguments for God's existence from non-religious premises. (2) To Unitarianism—particularly the more common non-theistic forms—these points apply far less than to many other religions. There may indeed be forms of Unitarianism and other broadly religious outlooks that are not plausibly considered religions—though they would be *religious*, in the sense John Dewey noted, in which appropriate attitudes, e.g. of reverence, can mark a perspective as religious even if it is not part of *a religion*. Dewey's distinction among the notions of religion, the religious, and *a* religion is a major topic of definition that I cannot address directly in this essay.

44. In "Acting from Virtue," cited above, I provide an account of such action which supports the conception of it employed here.

45. Our voice is, however, likely to be also determined *in part* by what we say, and other things equal, a civic voice is not fully achieved if one is proposing religious reasons as grounds for public policy decisions. It may be possible, however, to present such reasons in a context that preserves a certain balance, e.g. by noting that, in addition to sufficient secular reasons for a piece of legislation such as permitting state aid to handicapped children in religious schools, many religious citizens will feel better able to provide for their children services they believe God requires. Thus, the emphasis on achieving a proper civic voice as part of civic virtue leads to no simple rule about the admissible content of advocacy of laws or public policies.

46. One has a voice as a writer and can have a civic voice as such. In some ways the voice of a writer is less easily, in some more easily, discerned; but the same general points seem to hold. It should also be noted that the need for a civic voice is greater in some roles and situations than others, e.g. greater in judicial decisions than in legislative discussions, greater there than in campaign speeches, and greater

there than in discussions of political issues in settings where individuals are infor-mally meeting in a public place. Among the various helpful treatments of this matter are Rawls, *Political Liberalism*, especially Lecture 6, and Greenawalt, *Private Con-sciences*, especially chaps. 13–15.

47. Rawls is not, however, as restrictive here as some of his readers may have thought. He says, e.g., that "Public reason . . . asks of us that the balance of those values we hold to be reasonable in a particular case is a balance we sincerely think can be seen to be reasonable by others . . . The only comprehensive doctrines that do not accord with public reason on a given question are those that cannot support a reasonable balance of political values . . . Certain reasonable comprehensive views fail to do this in some cases . . ." (*Political Liberalism*, 253).

48. For a detailed discussion of Rawls's restrictions, particularly as they bear on whether he is in the end an "Enlightenment liberal," see Jean Hampton, "The Common Faith of Liberalism," *Pacific Philosophical Quarterly* 75, nos. 3–4 (1994): pp. 186–216. Other recent critical discussions of value are Jürgen Habermas, "Rec-onciliation through the Public Use of Reason: Remarks on John Rawls's *Political Liberalism*," *Journal of Philosophy* 92, no. 3 (1995): pp. 109–31 (replied to by Rawls in the same issue, 132–80); and Joshua Cohen, "A More Democratic Liberalism," *Michigan Law Review* 92 (1994): pp. 1503–46. For criticism of both Rawls's and my views on the constraints appropriate to public political behavior, see Michael J. Perry, *Religion in Politics*, cited above.

49. For a quite different perspective see Michael J. Perry, cited above, wherein he argues that legislators in particular should give all the relevant arguments that they take seriously and indeed all the credible arguments that might incline a citizen to support a political choice at issue (chap. 2), and that religious arguments should be offered in public policy matters in order to test those arguments (Introduction and chap. 1). This view is particularly interesting given Perry's view that the con-clusion of a good religious argument, at least for government coercion, can always be supported by an equally plausible secular argument.

50. This and other claims about virtue in this paper are defended, at least implic-itly, in my "Acting from Virtue," cited above.

51. The notion of institutional citizenship needs explication, but I think it is significantly analogous to individual citizenship, though unlike an individual citizen a church has its own citizens—indeed, citizens forming a *community* rather than merely a group. There is a serious challenge here which the notion of institutional citizenship can meet only in part: according to Gerald Frug, as interpreted by Jean Bethke Elshtain, "American liberal thought and practice have no robust way to thematize entities intermediate between the state and the individual." See her "Catholic Social Thought, the City, and Liberal America," in *Catholicism, Liberal-ism, and Communitarianism*, eds. Kenneth L. Grasso, Gerard V. Bradley, and Robert P. Hunt (Lanham, MD: Rowman & Littlefield, 1995), p. 109 and, for an indication of her own perspective, pp. 111–12. A number of the essays in this volume also bear on the problem. Christopher Wolfe's "Subsidiarity: The 'Other' Ground of Limited Government" and Michelle Watkins and Ralph McInerny's "Jacques Maritain and the Rapprochement of Liberalism and Communitarianism" may be especially pertinent to the problem and to this essay in general.

52. Nothing less than the holism-individualism issue lurks here, the problem of whether wholes such as social groups are more than the individuals composing

them and their interrelations; for our purposes an individualistic reading of the principle is best, but the normative issues could be similarly treated if one plausibly formulated the principle as applying directly to institutions as such.

53. If the obligation is moral, it is presumably not contingent on churches' being committed to good institutional citizenship: that commitment itself would presumably be an institutional prima facie moral obligation. Moreover, at least if the obligation is moral I would take its prima facie character to imply not just that there is a reason for the conduct in question but that when that reason is overridden there should be an appropriate explanation, say in terms of one relevant value's outweighing another in the context, as illustrated by the case in which resisting tyranny justifies direct political action by a church.

54. I exclude those laws and policies essential for the existence of civil society of any kind, say the prohibitions of murder, rape, and theft. Details of these laws, say of the schedule of punishments, may be political issues in the relevant narrow sense, but the need for such laws in not an issue in that sense.

55. Again, Stephen Carter nicely expresses part of my point: of a young minister he once heard who preached in detail about El Salvador, he says, "For her, politics should lead faith, rather than the other way around—a proposition that is by no means the special reserve of the left. Her sermon, like many that were preached in support of Ronald Reagan's presidential candidacy, exemplified the problem of the political tail wagging the scriptural dog" (op. cit., p. 69). I differ with Carter, however, on how religious motivation should enter politics: the religious dog should be joined by a secular dog, sufficient for the task even if less important to the citizen and less vociferous than its religious companion. Given theo-ethical equilibrium, the two will pull together.

56. For valuable discussion of the general problem here see David Hollenbach, S. J., "The Political Role of Religion: Civil Society and Culture," *San Diego Law Review* 30, no. 4 (1993): pp. 877–901. At one point he says,

[S]ome fundamentalist Christians draw policy conclusions about the rights of homosexuals or about prayer in the public schools directly from the *Bible* . . . Some more conservative Catholics regard the legal banning of abortion as similarly entailed by the moral teachings of the pope and the Catholic bishops. From what has been said above about the need for believers to enter into dialogue with others in society as they develop their vision of the larger meaning of the social good and its consequences for policy, it is evident that I do not accept this understanding of the relation between religious belief and policy conclusions as immediate and direct. Roman Catholic thought, like much Protestant thought as well, maintains that religious belief must be complemented by the careful use of human reasoning, both philosophical and social-scientific, in the effort to reach decisions about policy that are both religiously and humanly adequate. (898)

57. Essentially this objection has been posed by Paul Weithman, and in responding to it I draw on my "Religious Commitment and Secular Reason: A Reply to Professor Weithman," *Philosophy & Public Affairs* 20, no. 1 (1991): pp. 66–76. For a more detailed statement of his view see his "Taking Rites Seriously," *Pacific Philosophical Quarterly* 73, nos. 3–4 (1994): pp. 272–94.

58. The determination of evidential adequacy is also a difficult matter, but is not

peculiar to my position on religious and politics: any plausible political philosophy must employ some such notion. It is perhaps some help to say that standard deductive and inductive logic are highly relevant, as is whatever logic of moral discourse there may be that goes beyond them.

59. A number of recent writers have commented on this, including Carter, op. cit., and Quinn, op. cit. For discussion of the putative "marginalization" and "privatization" of religion in the United States see Theodore Y. Blumoff, "The New Religionists' Social Gospel: On the Rhetoric and Reality of Religions' Marginalization' in Public Life," forthcoming.

60. Here one can be conscientiously mistaken: one can falsely but excusably believe a reason to be secular.

61. Paul J. Weithman, in "The Separation of Church and State: Some Questions for Professor Audi," *Philosophy & Public Affairs* 20, no. 1 (1991): pp. 62–65, and others have questioned how feasible it is to try to follow the principle of secular rationale. See also Lawrence B. Solum, "Faith and Justice," *DePaul Law Review* 39, no. 4 (1990): pp. 1083–1106, especially 1089–92. Also relevant is Weithman's "Rawlsian Liberalism and the Privatization of Religion: Three Theological Objections Considered," *Journal of Religious Ethics* 22, no. 1 (1994): pp. 3–28. The above is only the beginning of a reply to such worries. For another pertinent discussion see Jonathan Jacobs, "Theism and Moral Objectivity," *American Catholic Philosophical Quarterly* 66, no. 4 (1992).

62. One might think that a person must have *some* motivating reason for a belief or action. But this is not so, if we distinguish reasons from causes or, more subtly, reasons *for which* one believes or acts from mere (explanatory) *reasons why* one does: wishful thinking is a non-rational source of beliefs, and actions not performed intentionally need not be done for a reason, as where one quite unwittingly offends someone.

63. This result is suggested to be implicit in my view in Quinn, "Political Liberalisms and their Exclusions of the Religious," cited above, p. 36.

64. There are many issues here. Some are addressed in "The Separation of Church and State and the Obligations of Citizenship" and "The Place of Religious Argument in a Free and Democratic Society," cited above. Kent Greenawalt discusses the issues in *Religious Convictions and Political Choice* and *Private Consciences and Public Reasons*, both cited above.

65. The notion of neutrality is also informatively discussed by Rawls, op. cit., and Carter, op. cit.; see also Robert van Wyk, "Liberalism, Religion, and Politics," *Public Affairs Quarterly* 1, no. 3 (1987): pp. 59–76, and "Liberalism, Religion, and Politics Again: A Reply to Gordon Graham," *Journal of Social Philosophy* 25, no. 3 (1994): pp. 153–64. (Some of van Wyk's criticism of my view is at least implicitly answered in this essay.)

66. The Declaration of Independence is one famous document supporting liberal democracy that seems to imply otherwise; but I am not certain that it must be so read, nor do I take it to be as authoritative on this matter as the work of, say, John Stuart Mill.

67. This point (among many others relevant to this paper) is brought out by Kent Greenawalt in *Private Consciences and Public Reasons*, cited above.

68. This essay has benefited from discussions at the University of Notre Dame Conference on Liberalism and Religion in 1996, from audience discussions at the

Center for Ethics at Emory University, the University of Memphis, and Vanderbilt University, and from comments by James Fowler, Lenn Goodman, Kent Greenawalt, James Gustafson, Timothy Jackson, Hugh McCann, Michael Perry, Laurie Piper, Louis Pojman, Philip Quinn, Jeff Spinner-Halev, Mark Timmons, Mark van Roojen, Paul Weithman, and especially Nicholas Wolterstorff. I am also grateful for support from the Pew Foundation and the University of Nebraska, Lincoln.

THE ROLE OF RELIGION IN DECISION AND DISCUSSION OF POLITICAL ISSUES

Nicholas Wolterstorff

The Role of Citizen and Its Ethic

A most unusual form of state emerged in the early modern period in the West: liberal democracy. Nothing of the sort was known before. Though such states are now sufficiently common to be familiar to all who read these words, they are still far from universal.

Characteristic of liberal democracies, though not peculiar to them, is that they have *citizens*, not merely *subjects*. My principal topic in the following pages is the role of citizen in a liberal democracy: how that role should be performed. I will not by any means have the entirety of that role in mind, however. All my attention will be concentrated on one rather narrow, but important and intensely controversial, aspect of what goes into being a good citizen of a liberal democracy. It will be liberal democracy as we find it in the present-day United States that I will mainly have in view. Though some aspects of the role of citizen in a liberal democracy remain constant across all liberal democracies at all stages in their history, I wish to attend not only to such constants, but also to how the role is best performed here and now.

I assume that there is such a social role as that of citizen in a liberal democracy. Each of us is, as it were, a player in an evolving drama. In that drama, we each play many social roles, and many of us play the same role. Connected with each such role—so, too, then with the role of citizen—are rights and duties and mutual expectations. And beyond rights and duties, there are better and worse ways of playing the role—including, again, that of citizen. These roles are social artifacts; our knowing how to play them is the consequence of social learning. We are neither born with this knowledge, nor is it the automatic consequence of arriving at a certain level of biological maturity. In the course of our learning to play some such role, we learn the rights and duties pertaining thereto and some of the better and worse ways of playing the role—though we also learn, along the way, that at many points there is dispute rather than agreement as to what those duties are and the better and worse ways of carrying them out.

Though it is always possible to repudiate some social role, or deliberately to play it very badly, for many roles it is not a mere matter of choice whether one will or will not play them. It is expected that one will. Often it is not merely expected; it is regarded as obligatory that one do so. For example, if one becomes a father, then, other things being equal, it is not only expected that one will play the role of father; it is generally viewed as a matter of obligation that one do so. Naturally, one may choose to play the role of father in a new and different way, not as it has customarily been done, but that is a different matter. More radically, one may refuse to play the role of father not out of laxness but on the ground that somehow it would be wrong of one to do so, or, more moderately, on the ground that biological fatherhood carries with it no obligation to play the social role of father.

No doubt there are some people who, though citizens of liberal democracies, want as little as possible to do with playing the role of citizen. Usually indifference will be the cause. But it may well be that some people have moral scruples against playing the role any more than absolutely necessary. I will have relatively little to say about the extent to which citizens of liberal democracies are obligated to play the role of citizen; my attention will be focused almost entirely on that role itself. It is natural to wonder whether this sort of abstraction is possible—and if possible, desirable. I think it is both. It is quite possible to consider, say, the role of bishop in the Orthodox church of the thirteenth century without asking whether it was good that this or that person—or indeed, any person—played that role; for certain purposes it is not only possible but helpful to consider that role abstractly.

A common theme in the writings of those who have *theorized* about liberal democracy, going back into the late seventeenth century when liberal democracies were just beginning to emerge, is that a good citizen (and functionary) of a liberal democracy will impose certain *epistemological* restraints on the manner in which he decides and/or debates political issues; in his deciding and/or debating, he will refrain from letting reasons of a certain sort be determinative. Specifically, a common theme has been that a good citizen of a liberal democracy will refrain from allowing religious reasons to be determinative when deciding and/or debating political issues of certain sorts—or perhaps of any sort whatsoever, unless, perchance, those religious reasons are themselves held for reasons of the acceptable sort. Obviously, there will be other restraints as well on the decisions and discourse of the good citizen in a liberal democracy, restraints of content, for example. The good citizen of a liberal democracy (whose citizenry is religiously diverse) will refrain from advocating that only Presbyterians be permitted to hold office. My topic in the pages that follow is that proposed epistemological restraint. Is it indeed a requirement of being a good citizen in a liberal democracy that one's religion not be determinative of one's decisions on political issues, and/or that it not be determinative of the case one makes to others in favor of one's decision?

What Is a Liberal Democracy?

I had better take a moment to explain what I mean by liberal democracy. Though it is entirely possible for liberal democracy to be the form of governance in a society all of whose members share the same religion, much—though by no means all—of the *point* of liberal democracy would be missing in such a situation. Liberal democracy is in good measure a mode of governance relevant to those societies in which different religions are represented—and not only different religions, but different comprehensive perspectives on reality, the good life, and human destiny. Indeed, liberal democracy originated as a solution to the religious conflicts ravaging English society in the seventeenth century.

Liberal democracy is that mode of governance that grants to all people within the territory of its governance equal protection under law, that grants to its citizens equal freedom in law to live out their lives as they see fit, and that requires of the state that it be neutral as among all the religions and comprehensive perspectives represented in society. *Equal protection* under law for all people, *equal freedom* in law for all citizens, and *neutrality* on the part of the state with respect to the diversity of religions and comprehensive perspectives—those are the core ideas. Along with them is one immensely important addition: The governance of society is ultimately vested in the normal law-abiding adult citizens of society, and at the point of ultimate vesting, each such citizen has equal voice. Normally this voice is exercised by voting for office bearers and for options in referenda.

Liberal democracy, so defined, is an ideal type. For one thing, exemplification of the type requires decisions at a multitude of different points, and often it is not clear exactly what the decisions ought to be concerning the arrangements and practices necessary for equal protection, equal freedom, equal voice, and state neutrality. Thus it is that even among those who embrace the type, there is a great deal of controversy. But second, it is also an ideal type because, even on matters where the implications are clear, nowhere is it fully exemplified; exemplification of the type in any particular society is never anything more than approximate. No society is anything more than *more or less* a liberal democracy.

This can be seen from two distinct angles. Full exemplification is at certain points regarded as undesirable, even among those who embrace the type. Suppose that all normal law-abiding adult citizens in the state of New York have equal voice in the selection of their U.S. senators, and that all such citizens in the state of Rhode Island likewise have equal voice in the selection of their U.S. senators. Nonetheless, the extreme disparity of population in these two states results in an obvious inequality of voice of a certain sort when the senators of these two states take their seats in Congress. The composers of the U.S. Constitution regarded such disparity of voice as desirable; probably most citizens of the United States continue to do so. Second, countries such as the United States have been on a historical trajectory toward exemplifying more and more fully the ideal of liberal democracy, without yet being anywhere near doing so fully. For a long time, only white adult males—initially, white male *landholders*—enjoyed equal protection, freedom, and voice. Next, it was white adult males and females, then adults generally. The point is that the liberal-democratic ideal has had to win its way slowly in societies that were already structured along other lines, and against countervailing ideals and convictions.

Someone might question whether the Idea of liberal democracy really has *functioned as an ideal*—as those last words of mine suggest. As to history, it might be said that nothing more has been at work than the struggle of various groups to achieve their interests. And as to argumentation, it might be said that the controversies that have characterized liberal democracies have not been controversies over how to embody in history those big ideas of equal protection, equal freedom, equal voice, and state neutrality, but detailed disputes over how to legislate and adjudicate in particular cases. The parties to such disputes may well have tossed in references to 'big ideas' such as liberty and equality, but that was mere rhetoric, sincere or insincere as the case may be. What was actually involved was nothing else than the attempt to secure one's interests.

This objection is on to something; otherwise it would not have the plausibility that undoubtedly it does have. Nonetheless, I do not concede the main point. In my judgment, many of our controversies in the United States really have been controversies over the attempt to think through what would constitute equal protection, freedom, and voice in particular cases. And present in the mix of the many factors that motivate us, individually and collectively, has been the ideal of achieving a society of equal protection, freedom, and voice. That ideal has had to compete with other considerations; often it has lost, and often it continues to lose, the competition. But it is and has been a member of the competition, and sometimes it wins. Sometimes we have acted as we have so as to bring the ideal closer to earth.

It may help if we dwell for a moment on how remarkable this Idea of liberal democracy is and how even more remarkable it is that certain societies should come rather close to embodying the Idea. Nobody who is at all reflective believes that all religions and comprehensive perspectives in contemporary American society are equally correct and beneficial. How could they be, since on many points they flagrantly contradict each other? And should anyone say that correctness is not at issue when it comes to religions and comprehensive perspectives, that claim itself contradicts all those religions and perspectives that incorporate the conviction that correctness is at issue. But if we each believe that there are religions and perspectives present in society that are false and deleterious, it is remarkable that we should nonetheless advocate granting equal freedom to all, and remarkable likewise that we should insist that the state be neutral as among all these competing religions. Almost always in the past, societies have coped with religious diversity by granting hegemony to one among the many religions, confining members of the other religions to millets, ghettos, and so forth. It is also remarkable that we should consent to place ultimate political power in the hands of 'the people,' and that we should be willing to let 'the people' exercise that power by granting to all normal adult law-abiding citizens equal voice within voting schemes judged more or less fair. Obviously, some people are much wiser on political matters than others; why give the foolish as much voice as the wise?

The Liberal Position

A society in which all people are accorded equal protection under the law, in which all citizens are granted equal freedom in law to live their lives as they see fit, in which all normal adults are accorded equal voice within fair voting schemes, and in which the state is neutral as among the religions and comprehensive perspectives present in society—such a society needs a set of laws to govern the interactions among its members. Arriving at such laws will typically be a multi-stage process: citizens voting for legislators, citizens speaking out in public for and against proposed laws, legislators passing laws, judges applying laws, citizens voting on referenda, and so forth. At every stage, the question arises: on what basis are decisions to be made and debates to be conducted, whether by citizens or officials? What I shall call 'the liberal position' is one among several competing answers to this question. I do, I readily admit, court confusion in speaking both about *liberal democratic society*, and about *the liberal position*. But the term 'liberal' is so well established in both uses that innovation seems misguided.

One answer to our question—not the liberal position, let me say at once—is that the basis for all such decisions and debates on the part of citizens is simply perceived self-interest. Citizens make up their minds on the basis of perceived self interest, they debate with their fellow citizens on that basis, and they act politically on that basis. They vote their perceived self-interest, and they do what they can—in conformity with the laws, of course—to get the legislators to vote their way. The legislators then settle on such trade-offs as they anticipate will win them election next time around. On this view, liberal politics is, through and through, competition among interests—a historically novel arrangement for satisfying the ever-shifting majority. On this view, the role of citizen in a liberal democracy really does not come to much with respect to the obligations attaching thereto.

That, as I say, is not the liberal position. The liberal position is that the proper goal of political action in a liberal democratic society, on the part of citizens and officials alike, is *justice*. The end at which the good citizen aims in her deliberations, decisions, actions, and debates on political issues is that the rules governing our social interaction secure justice.

And what is the appropriate source of the factual and moral convictions on the basis of which determinations of justice are to be made? That, for the person who embraces the liberal position, is the central question. Definitive of the position is a negation at this point: citizens (and officials) *are not* to base their decisions and/or debates concerning political issues on their religious convictions. When it comes to such activities, they are to allow their religious convictions to idle. They are to base their political decisions and their political debate in the public space on the principles yielded by some source *independent of* any and all of the religious perspectives to be found in society. To this, the liberal adds one important qualification and one important addendum. The qualification is this: should the independent source itself yield convictions that are appropriately classified as 'religious,' these may be used in decision and debate. The point is that no 'positive' religion is to be used thus. The addendum is this: the source must be such that it is *fair* to insist that everybody base his or her political decisions, as well as public political debates, on the principles yielded by that source. This addendum eliminates what would otherwise be obvious candidates for the political basis. A good many of the nationalisms of the contemporary world are rich and thick enough to serve as the basis of the political decisions and debates of the members of society; in addition, they are often relatively independent of the religions to be found in the society. But rarely if ever will it be fair to insist that the life of the polity be based on some nationalism, because it is no longer ever true that all the citizens of a single polity belong to the same nation, the same 'people.'

Given this understanding of what I have called 'the liberal position,' it turns out that what is in view here is not one position, but *a family* of positions, with the members of the family differing along a number of distinct strands of similarity and difference. This must be kept in mind in all that follows; my phrase 'the liberal position' is only a convenient name for the *family* of liberal *positions*.

What leaps to mind at once is that, since the family is picked out with a negation, it is possible for different members of the family to go beyond the shared negation with different positive suggestions as to the nature of the independent source. This possibility has in fact been actualized. Some have argued that the basis should be 'publicly accessible reasons'; others have argued that it should be 'secular reasons'; yet others have argued that it should be reasons derived from the shared political culture of one's liberal democracy. Furthermore, it is possible to expand or contract the negation itself, thereby gaining yet additional members of the family. As to expansion: one might hold that it is not only out of order to base one's political decisions and debates on one's *religion*; it is equally out of order, for those who are not religious, to base their decisions and debates on their non-religious comprehensive perspectives. And as to contraction: One might hold that it is acceptable to base one's political decisions and debates on religious reasons if those reasons satisfy some qualification in addition to the one already mentioned—if, for example, those religious reasons are non-sectarian.

It will prove important to have in view some of the other axes along which members of that family which constitutes the liberal position resemble and differ from each other. Whereas some members of the family impose the same restraint on personal decision and public debate alike, others allow a person to decide issues for himself as he wishes, and impose the restraint only on the reasons one offers in public debate. Again, the restraints that some propose are meant for all political issues, whereas others, such as Rawls, intend their restraints only for "constitutional issues" and "matters of basic justice." And yet again, the proposals differ with respect to how one's non-religious reasons for or against some political position are to be related to one's religious reasons, should one have religious reasons. Some say that it is acceptable for one's religious reasons to motivate one's decision or action, provided that one also has a non-religious reason that would be sufficient, by itself, as motive; others insist that whatever religious reasons one may have ought not to play any motivating role at all. Some insist that one should never use religious reasons in public debate; others hold that it is acceptable to do so, provided one is both able and ready to offer non-religious reasons. Lastly, there is, as one would expect, considerable divergence among the members of the family as to how religious reasons are to be identified, with the consequence that a reason that is disallowed as religious on one proposal is permitted as non-religious on another.

What unites this buzzing variety of positions into one family of liberal positions is that they all propose a restraint on the use of religious reasons in deciding and/or debating political issues. That is the heart of the matter. The positions of interest to us here are those that propose a *significant* restraint. In principle, a proposed restraint on religious reasons might be so narrow in its application that it almost never applies to anybody. Such a position would be of no interest to us here—given the presence of so many big fish in the pond. In a specific practical situation, it might be not only interesting but desperately important.

Though I am taking the *religious-reason restraint* to be, by itself, definitive of what I mean by 'the liberal position,' it should be noted that it is typical of those who propose significant versions of this restraint also to embrace a certain understanding of the neutrality that the state in a liberal democracy is supposed to exercise with respect to the religions present in that society. We may call it the

separation interpretation. It is possible to interpret the neutrality pro-
viso as requiring that government and its agents treat all religions
impartially. That is not the interpretation that those who hold a significant version of the liberal position typically adopt. The position
that the liberal typically adopts is rather that government is to do
nothing to advance or hinder any religion. The difference between
these two interpretations, the *impartiality* interpretation and the *separation* interpretation, can most easily be seen by taking note of the
difference in result on the issue of state aid to schools with a religious
orientation. The impartiality position says that if the state aids any
school, it must aid all schools, and aid them all equitably—no matter
what their religious orientation, if any. The separation position says
that the state is to aid no school whose orientation is religious. The
First Amendment in the United States Bill of Rights specifies that
the government shall neither establish any religion, nor infringe on
the free exercise of any. That formulation is ambiguous as between
the impartiality and the separation positions. The U.S. Supreme
Court, in its decisions over the past fifty years, has nonetheless consistently interpreted the amendment as an affirmation of the separation position. It has ruled as if Jefferson's *wall of separation* metaphor
had been incorporated into the Constitution. Possibly the recent
Virginia v. Rosenberger decision indicates a change in direction.

The Ethic of the Citizen and Restraints on Reasons

It is easy to see why and how the role of citizen in a liberal
democracy imposes restraints on the legislation that one advocates.
There are probably some evangelical Christians who believe that
American society would be better off if only evangelical Christians
were allowed to vote and hold office. But such an arrangement
would be flamboyantly out of accord with the Idea of liberal democracy. Of course, such a person might also be of the view that liberal
democracy should be abolished. But our topic, let us be reminded,
is not whether American society, or any other, should be liberal
democratic in form, nor whether it is a good thing that citizens of

this or any other liberal democracy play the role of citizen. Our topic is instead the contours of that role of citizen.

Once again, then, it is obvious that the role of citizen involves restraints on the legislation advocated. But what is the rationale for *epistemological* restraints on the decisions and debates of citizens? That is, why should epistemological restraints be laid on a person *when the legislation advocated by that person does not violate the restraints on content?* What difference does it make what reasons citizens use in making their decisions and conducting their debates, if the positions they advocate do not violate the Idea of liberal democracy? And in particular, why should *religious* reasons (which are not derived from the independent source) be singled out for exclusion?

Not only is it not at once evident what rationale there might be for proposing such a restraint, but on the face of it, there is something profoundly paradoxical about the suggestion that the role of citizen in a liberal democracy includes this restraint. The restraint appears, on the face of it, to violate the equal freedom component within the Idea of liberal democracy. On the face of it, the Idea of liberal democracy implies the *absence* of any such restraint. A significant part of how some citizens exercise their religion is that their decisions and debates on political issues are in good measure based on their religious convictions. Using their religious convictions in making their decisions and conducting their debates on political issues is part of what constitutes conducting their lives as they see fit. What is going on here? The liberal position—restraint on religious reasons—appears to be in flagrant conflict with the Idea of liberal democracy.

Is it perhaps the liberal position that at this point it is best not to exemplify the Idea of liberal democracy? If so, then, speaking strictly, the liberal position is not that this epistemological restraint belongs to the role of citizen in a liberal democracy, but that at this point the subjects of the state should not play that role. At this point, it is best that the society not exemplify the Idea of liberal democracy. Or is the clue, perhaps, to be found in the 'equal' of the phrase, "equal freedom to live one's life as one sees fit"? Though the restraint appears to be imposed non-equitably, singling out, as it does, *religious* reasons, when only some citizens would ever use such reasons, does it prove, on scrutiny, to preserve *equality* of freedom?

Are Religious Reasons too Dangerous to Permit?

One reason regularly cited, more in the past than now, for insisting that citizens not use religious reasons for their decisions and/ or debates on political issues (and for adopting the separation rather than the impartiality interpretation of state neutrality) is that it is simply too dangerous, in a situation of religious pluralism, to allow religion to intrude into politics in this way. Religion stirs up too many passions. The amity of society will be endangered and, thereby, the stability and endurance of the state. By analogy: many of us have found ourselves in family situations where the only way to preserve peace in the family was for everyone to agree not to bring up certain religious issues—or certain political issues! So too: best that all citizens refrain from citing religious reasons in public debate on political issues—that instead they make use exclusively of reasons derived from some equitable independent source.

And what about using religious reasons to make up one's own mind on political issues? Picture the situation if that is permitted and practiced, while the use of religious reasons in public discussion is prohibited. Many citizens would arrive at their views on political issues by reasoning from their religious convictions. Then, however, when they get together in discussion and debate, they conceal that these are their reasons; instead they offer reasons derived from the independent source.

Social peace would admittedly not be endangered by this sort of practice. But for one thing, it is patently unrealistic as a proposal. Most people who reasoned from their religion in making up their mind on political issues would lack the intellectual imagination required for reasoning to the same position from premises derived from the independent source. Probably in many cases it just could not be done; in the absence of detailed information about the religion, on the one hand, and about the independent source, on the other, we do not actually know. But even if it could be done, it is appropriate to hesitate over the massive dissembling that would take place. Many members of society would hold their political views for religious reasons; then, in public, they would conceal this fact about themselves and offer quite distinct reasons.

In short, the most reasonable position in the region would seem to be that citizens should hold their political views for reasons derived from the independent source. Should some of the views thus held *also* be held for religious reasons, that would be acceptable; it would be a case of harmless overdetermination.

Let us be clear on the relation of this particular version of the liberal position to the Idea of liberal democracy. No attempt is made to *derive* this version of the position from the Idea; indeed, none is even made to show that the version is *compatible* with the Idea. Whether or not it is compatible, the argument is that citizens ought not to hold their views and conduct their debates concerning political issues on the basis of religious reasons. Should some citizen think otherwise, then, in this regard, he ought not to live out his life as he sees fit. Nobody has ever proposed enforcing this obligation by criminalizing such behavior; it would be enforced by social disapproval. And should it be the case that the restraint in question is imposed unequally, then this clear-and-present-danger argument proves in fact to be an argument for not exemplifying the Idea of liberal democracy at this point.

What about the argument itself: is it cogent? Of course, without a suggestion as to what the independent source is to be, we do not yet have a definite version of the liberal position. But let us consider all by itself this particular argument against the use of religious reasons in decisions and discussions on political issues.

Whether the argument is or is not cogent all depends, it seems to me, on the particular society one has in mind and the particular stage in the history of that society. For seventeenth-century England, it quite clearly was cogent: social peace did depend on getting citizens to stop invoking God, canonical scriptures, and religious authorities when discussing politics in public—to confine such invocations to discussions within their own confessional circles.

American society at the end of the twentieth century is a different matter. We now have behind us a long history of religious tolerance. There is plenty of passion in the politics of the present-day United States, but those passions are, for the most part, not attached

to such religious reasons as people might have for their political
positions, but to those political positions themselves: passionate feelings pro and con the so-called 'welfare state,' for example. More
generally: the slaughter, torture, and generalized brutality of our
century has mainly been conducted in the name of one or another
secular cause—nationalisms of many sorts, communism, fascism, pa-
triotisms of various kinds, economic hegemony. In seventeenth-
century Europe, human beings cared deeply about religion. In our
century, most have cared more deeply about various secular causes.
It would be dangerously myopic to focus one's attention on the
danger that religion poses to the polity while ignoring the equal or
greater danger posed by secular causes.

The other side of the matter is also worth mentioning. Many
of the social movements in the modern world that have moved societies in the direction of liberal democracy have been deeply and
explicitly religious in their orientation: the abolitionist movement
in nineteenth-century America, the civil rights movement in twen-
tieth-century America, the resistance movements in fascist Germany, in communist Eastern Europe, in apartheid South Africa.
These movements are often analyzed by Western academics and in-
tellectuals as if religion were nowhere in the picture. The assumption, presumably, is that religion plays no explanatory role in human
affairs and thus does not require mentioning. It is only an epiphe-
nomenon. The people in Leipzig assembled in a meeting space that
just happened to be a church to listen to inspiring speeches that just
happened to resemble sermons; they were led out into the streets in
protest marches by leaders who just happened to be pastors.[1] Black
people in Capetown were led on protest marches from the black
shanty-towns into the center of the city by men named Tutu and
Boesak—who just happened to be bishop and pastor, respectively,
and who just happened to use religious talk in their fiery speeches.
Thus does ideology conceal reality and distort scholarship! Even the
free and equal doctrine, which lies at the very heart of liberal democracy, had religious roots—in Protestant dissent of the seventeenth century.

Locke's Version of the Liberal Position

When we now move on to consider other arguments that have
been offered for the view that the role of citizen in a liberal democ-

racy includes a restraint on the use of religious reasons, we shall·
want at the same time to consider what is being proposed as the
independent source of principles to serve as basis for decisions and
discussions on political issues. Should that independent source be
inadequately identified, prove incapable of doing the work asked of
it, or be of such a nature that it would be unfair to ask of all citizens
that they use it in their decisions and discussions on political issues,
then the version as a whole will be unacceptable, no matter how
cogent the argument against the use of religious reasons might be,
considered alone. Of course, a version might also founder on one
and another detail; for example, it might refuse to allow the use of
religious reasons in making decisions even when they do nothing
more than overdetermine the decision, whereas, given the fundamental rationale of the version, such use of religious reasons ought
to be allowed. On this occasion I will skip lightly over such details,
focusing on the rationale offered for the restraint on religious reasons, and on the independent basis proposed as replacement.

Let me now be explicit—the view that I will be defending is
that the liberal position is unacceptable in all its versions. It is unacceptable not because none of the extant versions happens to get all
the details right, but unacceptable because no rationale offered for
the restraint is cogent, and no independent source meets the demands.

Let me make clear that it is not the Idea of liberal democracy
that I oppose; to the contrary, I firmly embrace it. What I oppose is
the liberal position: the thesis that the role of citizen in a liberal democracy includes a restraint on the use of reasons, derived from
one's religion, for one's decisions and discussions on political issues,
and a requirement that citizens instead use an independent source.
In due course I will explain and defend my alternative to the liberal
position, which I will be calling the *consocial* position. I contend that
the consocial position is fully harmonious with the Idea of liberal
democracy.

We have no option but to make a choice from among the multiplicity of different versions of the liberal position. I propose confining myself to the most influential of the traditional versions, that
of John Locke, and to the most influential of the contemporary versions, that of John Rawls. All the important options and issues concerning rationale and independent sources will come up.[2]

John Locke was one of the first, and remains one of the greatest, theorists of liberal democracy. Locke did not explicitly distinguish between the use of religious reasons in deciding political issues for oneself and the use of such reasons in discussing political issues in public. His attention was focused entirely on the proper basis for the formation of political convictions; it never occurred to him that anything different, or even additional, had to be said about reasons that one offers in the public space. Even the distinction between public and private, which for a long time now has played a fundamental role in almost all versions of the liberal position, plays no role whatsoever in Locke's discussion. What Locke had to say about the proper source of principles to serve as a basis for political opinions was pretty much a straightforward implication of his general epistemology; it is that epistemology, then, that we must spend most of our time trying to get in hand.[3]

Though Locke had a good deal to say about knowledge, the focus of his attention was not on that but on *belief*. This contrast, *not knowledge, but belief*, will be puzzling to students of contemporary epistemology in the analytic tradition, since knowledge is standardly treated there not as something *other* than belief but as a *species* of belief: knowledge is that species of belief whose propositional content is true, whose status is justification (or warrant), and so forth. But that is not how Locke was thinking of knowledge—nor indeed how most of the tradition before him thought of knowledge. Whereas Locke described belief as *taking some proposition to be true*, he understood knowledge as consisting in *awareness* of some entity or fact—"perception," as he regularly called it. He acknowledged that awareness of some fact regularly evokes belief of the corresponding proposition, but it was the former, not the latter, that he identified as knowledge.

What mainly drew Locke's attention, when reflecting on belief, was that our beliefs are often false; from there he moved on, with never a hesitation in his skip, to affirm that we are all under obligation to govern and regulate our belief-forming faculties with the aim of improving the proportion of truth to falsehood in their output.

It will be worth taking a moment to set Locke's thought here within a somewhat broader context. In everyday life we all take for granted that beliefs have merits and defects, and that these merits and defects are of various sorts. One of the most important distinctions is between those merits and defects that have nothing to do with truth, and those that are what one might call 'truth-relevant.' The merit of *making one feel happy* is an example of the former. Perhaps the belief that you passed the exam is what has put you in a happy mood; its doing so had nothing at all to do with its truth. As to truth-relevant merits: the most obvious example—all too obvious—is truth itself. What is especially important to notice, however, is the multiplicity and diversity of truth-relevant merits and defects. In addition to 'truth,' writers on these matters have used the following adjectives assuming that they were thereby picking out truth-relevant merits in beliefs: 'justified,' 'warranted,' 'rational,' 'reliably formed,' 'scientific,' 'self-evident,' and—to cut the list short—'certain.' I said that writers on these matters have used these adjectives *assuming* that they were picking out truth-relevant merits; I did not say that they were in fact picking out such merits. My reason for caution is my conviction that some adjectives on the list—'justified' and 'rational' in particular—are incurably vague, and that all too often it is impossible to know what merit the writer was picking out with the adjective because there really was not any one that he was picking out. Debates about *the nature of justification* and *the nature of rationality* have usually, for that reason, been utterly futile. But that beliefs do come with a variety of truth-relevant merits, and that often we do pick out one or another of them—of this there can be no doubt.

Among such merits is what I shall call *entitlement*. Entitled beliefs are permitted beliefs. "You should have known better than to assume that half an hour was enough to allow for changing planes in O'Hare." "You should never have believed what he told you without also checking it out with his wife." We use such sentences to charge each other with holding beliefs that we are not entitled to hold, not permitted. Rather often, in recent academic writing on these matters, the adjective 'rational' is used as a synonym for 'entitled': a belief that one is entitled to hold is said to be a belief that it is rational for one to hold. For the reason indicated above, however, when speaking in my own voice I shall almost always abjure the use of the word 'rational.'

Locke, as I mentioned, was more interested in belief than in knowledge. Since knowledge, in his words, is "short and scanty," and would never be anything but that, mainly it fell on us human beings to regulate our belief-forming faculties, and to regulate them with the aim of believing what is true and of not believing what is false. Not only is it desirable that we do so; we have obligations to do so. It is on account of such obligations that the merit of entitlement enters the picture, and the demerit of non-entitlement. Not being entitled to some belief is grounded in the fact that one has failed at some point to fulfill one's obligations concerning the regulation of one's belief-forming faculties.

Locke set out then to formulate a criterion for entitlement in beliefs—or what in essentials comes to the same thing: he set out to formulate the deontological rules that hold for the governance of our belief-forming faculties. Not a *general* criterion for entitlement, however. Though much of Locke's rhetoric is universalistic, a number of passages, both in the *Essay Concerning Human Understanding* and in the *Conduct of the Understanding*, make clear that he had no interest whatsoever in offering a criterion of entitlement applicable to all beliefs. He was concerned exclusively with situations of maximal concernment—"concernment" being his word. That is, he was concerned exclusively with situations in which one is obligated to do *the best* to find out the truth of the matter, and to believe in accord with the results of one's endeavor. His strategy was to articulate a practice of inquiry whose competent employment constitutes, in his judgment, doing the best: the *optimal* practice of inquiry. It follows that, on matters of maximal concernment, one is entitled to one's belief (or non-belief) if and only if one has competently employed the optimal practice and believes or refrains from believing in a manner appropriate to the results of the employment.

Locke sometimes describes this (supposedly) optimal practice as "listening to the voice of Reason." At other times he describes it as "getting to the things themselves." The point of the latter formulation is that, by employing the practice, one gets to the things themselves *instead of resting content with what people tell one about the things*. One circumvents tradition.

The essential elements of the practice are easily described. We can think of it as having three stages. With some proposition in mind concerning the matter in question, one first collects evidence concerning the truth or falsehood of the proposition, this evidence to consist of a non-skewed and sufficiently ample set of beliefs that are certain for one because their propositional content corresponds directly to facts of which one is (or remembers having been) aware. Second, by the exercise of one's reason one determines the probability of the proposition on that evidence. And last, one adopts a level of confidence in the proposition corresponding to its probability on that evidence. To competently employ this practice, says Locke, is to do the human best.

Whether or not a matter is of maximal concernment to a person is a function of the whole contour of that person's obligations—the consequence of which is that what matters are of maximal concernment varies from person to person. Locke insisted on an extremely important limitation on this principle of variation, however. Matters of religion and morality are of maximal concernment to everybody. Nobody is entitled to hold his religious or moral convictions on the unverified say-so of someone else. Accordingly, everybody is obligated to employ the optimal practice on such matters.

Locke believed that by employing the practice, we could arrive at a very substantial body of moral truths. This is the *natural law*, which functions so pivotally in his *Second Treatise of Government.* Natural law, for Locke, simply *is* those moral truths that are accessible to human reason, unaided by divine revelation. And what he means by "human reason," in this context, is that optimal practice of inquiry, described above. Locke also believed that by employing the optimal practice, we could arrive at a substantial set of beliefs about God and could establish the reliability of the New Testament. Thereby we would gain a second mode of access to moral truth, because the teachings of Jesus include the fundamental tenets of natural law—and much more besides.

Locke was thus most definitely not a proponent of secularism. His thought was rather that when it comes to matters of morality and religion, it is the obligation of all of us to employ the optimal practice, thus to arrive at a 'rational' morality and a 'rational' religion. Rather than appealing to the moral and religious traditions into which we have been inducted, it is our obligation, by employing the optimal practice, to appeal solely to the deliverances of our generic human nature applied directly to the things themselves.

It follows that, when deciding and discussing political matters, we are not entitled to appeal to our own particular religious tradition. It would be wrong to do so. It would be wrong to appeal to one's own religious tradition whether or not the matter under consideration was political. That is not to say that everything we have come to believe, by virtue of being inducted into some religious and moral tradition, is off-limits in political debate. If, by employing that optimal practice, in which one supposedly makes use only of one's generically human capacities applied directly to the things themselves, one succeeds in arriving at some of the content of one's tradition, then one is entitled to appeal to that content in one's political decisions and discussions. But one is entitled to do so *only because* those religious and moral propositions are part of the yield of that optimal practice. Religious reasons *as such* are not excluded from decision and discussion, only those that are what I shall call 'uncertified.'

Locke's rationale for the restraint he proposes on the use of uncertified religious beliefs as reasons in decision and discussion on political issues is now eminently clear: we should not use uncertified religious beliefs in that manner because we should not even have such beliefs. We are not entitled to them. And if we should not even *have* them, then we should certainly not *use* them as reasons. Only beliefs that one is permitted to have are beliefs that one is permitted to use as reasons. Furthermore, the restraint is indubitably equitable; religion is not being subjected to an invidious classification. Though Locke certainly had his eye on the destructive consequences of using religion to argue about politics in the public square, the classification that is actually operative in the restraint he proposes is not that of religious versus non-religious beliefs, but that of entitled versus non-entitled beliefs. As it turns out, most of the religious beliefs that people actually hold are not entitled. But the same is true for most of the moral beliefs that people hold—whether or not those moral beliefs are intertwined with religion. Locke's fundamental thought is that the role of citizen in a liberal democracy incorporates the requirement that the beliefs one uses as reasons, in deciding and discussing political issues, be beliefs to which one is entitled. To this he adds a thesis about entitlement: one is only entitled to those moral and religious beliefs that are the output of one's adequate employment of the (supposedly) optimal practice.

The elegance of Locke's version of the liberal position is undeniable, and the explicitness of the underlying epistemology, admirable. All versions of the liberal position, with the exception of the clear-and-present-danger version, make crucial use of epistemological assumptions in what they say about acceptable versus non-acceptable reasons. Yet seldom is the epistemology brought up front and developed articulately. John Locke is one of the great and noble exceptions to this generalization.

But elegant and admirable though it be, Locke's version of the liberal position will not do—fundamentally because its underlying epistemology, though admirably articulated, is nonetheless untenable. Since almost no one today would contest that claim, my critique will be brief.[4]

In the first place, the rationale Locke offers for restraint on the use of religious reasons is defective. Locke holds that only if one holds one's religious beliefs for reasons of that highly specific sort that he specifies is one entitled to those beliefs. The development in recent years, at the intersection of philosophy of religion and epistemology, of what has come to be known as 'Reformed epistemology,' is a powerful attack on that claim.[5] *Decisive*, even—though I say this as one who has participated in the development. Not only is it not the case that one must hold one's religious beliefs for reasons of the Lockean sort to be entitled to them, it is not, in general, necessary that one hold them for any reasons at all. Something about the belief, the person, and the situation brings it about that the person is entitled to the belief. But that need not be another belief whose propositional content functions as reason for the religious belief. Entitlement simply does not effect the winnowing that Locke thought it would.

Second, the independent source that Locke proposed comes nowhere near yielding the beliefs necessary for making our political decisions and conducting our political discussions. That source, remember, was the practice that Locke thought to be optimal. Not only did Locke hold that moral truths, sufficient for our personal and communal lives, would be yielded by the recommended practice. He held that a *scientia* of morality was possible, comparable, so he held, to the already-extant *scientia* of mathematics. That is to say: he thought that it was possible, beginning with certitudes, to construct a *deductive* system of moral truths. Probability calculations need not enter the picture. And in Locke's system, let us recall, one is certain of a proposition on account of *being aware of* (or remembering having been aware of) the corresponding fact. Locke was heavily pressed, in his own day, to validate his bold claim by actually developing a science of morality. He conceded that he was incapable of doing so—though there is no evidence, in my judgment, that that concession was based on doubts about the possibility of the project. He simply thought that, elderly as he then was, he wasn't 'up to' it. The skepticism of the critics has by now been amply borne out, however: no one has ever developed a *scientia* of morality. Indeed, no one has ever succeeded in developing a system of morality by using the somewhat less demanding procedures of Locke's optimal practice. (Less demanding, in that probabilistic inferences are allowed in addition to deductive inferences.)

A third point of critique is worth adding, since the issues posed will prove relevant later in our discussion. Fundamental to Locke's strategy and vision was his conviction that communal traditions and individual say-so are endlessly productive of error. At points of 'concernment' that are maximal, we must all set aside all that we believe on the say-so of others and apply our generically human hard-wiring directly to 'the things themselves.' In his eyes, what made the practice of inquiry, which he recommended, optimal, was that, by employing it, we did exactly that. We got at 'the things themselves' by employing only our generically human hard-wiring.

In the penultimate chapter of the *Essay*, however, Locke offers a devastating critique of this visionary hope, apparently without realizing how devastating it is. The critique consists of a counter-example. Imagine, says Locke, a child reared in Roman Catholicism, who comes to accept as indubitable truth the doctrine of transubstantiation. Now in fact that doctrine, says Locke, is not only false, but self-evidently false. Nonetheless, the person reared in Catholicism does not believe that the doctrine is false, even when he grasps it as firmly as does Locke. Both he and Locke are aware of the proposition in question—in Locke's terminology, both he and Locke 'perceive' the proposition. In Locke's case, that perception immediately evokes disbelief of the proposition. In the case of the Catholic believer, it does not.

Why the difference? The answer, obviously, is that the Catholic person has been programmed in such a way that disbelief is not forthcoming even though he has the requisite 'perception.' That, anyway, is how Locke would describe the situation, had the terms 'hard-wiring' and 'programming' been available to him for metaphorical use. The Catholic person would of course return the favor and say that *Locke* had been programmed in such a way that the 'perception' did not evoke the belief. The picture with which Locke operated, in the main body of his *Essay*, was that we all come hardwired with belief-forming dispositions. These dispositions then get activated by certain experiences, the output being beliefs; these beliefs, unless they are simply forgotten, are then stored in memory. Among the experiences that evoke beliefs in us are people telling us things; we have a disposition to believe what people tell us. But since so much of what people tell us is false, when we are confronted with an issue of maximal concernment, best to ignore what they tell us, and simply make use of those belief-forming dispositions of ours that are activated by direct awareness of facts.

That, I say, is the picture with which Locke operated in the body of his work. In that penultimate chapter, a quite different picture puts in its appearance. The beliefs that we already have, however acquired, are not merely stored inertly in memory, waiting to be lifted out should the occasion arise. They become components in our programming. What determines whether I will believe the doctrine of transubstantiation, upon grasping it, is the beliefs that I bring with me to the enterprise. In forming beliefs in response to experience, I do not and cannot operate as a generic human being. I operate as a person with such-and-such a contour of beliefs, such-and-such a contour of affections, such-and-such a contour of habits and skills of attention—and so forth. What I come to believe is a function of my experience plus what I already believe. It is not just a function of my experience. The traditions into which we have been inducted cannot just be set on the shelf, cannot be circumvented. They have become components of ourselves as belief-forming agents: components of our programming. We live *inside* our traditions, not *alongside*.

Let me close my discussion of Locke by remarking that as long as the Lockean practice, or something like it, was widely thought to yield a substantial 'rational' religion, along with 'rational' evidence for the reliability of the Christian scriptures, American religious leaders were relatively content with the liberal position. That was the situation throughout the nineteenth century. It was when skepticism on those scores became widespread—impelled especially, in my judgment, by the emergence of Darwinian evolutionary theory and the rise of biblical criticism—that tensions began to mount between religious believers and defenders of the liberal position. That tension has in recent years become acute.

Rawls's Version of the Liberal Position

As was the case for Locke, the principal questions we want to answer in our exposition of John Rawls are these: What rationale does he offer for the restraint he proposes on religious reasons? What does he propose as the independent source? Is that source effectively identified, will it do the work asked of it, and is it fair to demand of religious people that they use this source, rather than their religion, as the basis of their decisions and discussions on political matters?

One way of interpreting Locke is to see him as urging the formation of a *new* comprehensive perspective on matters of religion, morality, and science—a properly grounded perspective, in competition with all those ungrounded perspectives that get handed down in tradition or devised by fancy. It is this new comprehensive perspective that is to serve as basis for our political decisions and discussions. Well aware of this classic liberal strategy, Rawls, in his recent book, *Political Liberalism*,[6] makes no bones about his conviction that "the question the dominant tradition has tried to answer has no answer; no comprehensive doctrine is appropriate as a political conception" (135). Not at least for a liberal democracy. In such a society, no one of the comprehensive doctrines can "secure the basis of social unity, nor can it provide the content of public reason on fundamental political questions" (134). One of the great merits of Rawls's discussion is that, under "comprehensive doctrines," he includes not only religions but comprehensive philosophies. In a liberal democracy, no comprehensive perspective—be it religious or not, be it of God and the good, or only of the good, be it an extant perspective or one newly devised—no comprehensive perspective can properly serve as the basis of decisions and discussions on fundamental political questions, nor would social unity be secured by allowing any one to function thus.

Much of what lies behind this claim on Rawls's part is chastened epistemology. Political liberalism, he says, must concede the existence in liberal democracies of a plurality of religions with adherents who are *entitled* to their adherence. And not just religions: "It must concede that there are many conflicting reasonable comprehensive doctrines with their conceptions of the good" (135). The test of entitlement does not pick out one from the diversity; neither can it serve as a guide for devising a new 'rational' religion, or some 'rational' secular perspective, which will then be the sole entitled member of the mix. "The political culture of a democratic society," says Rawls, "is always marked by a diversity of opposing and irreconcilable religious, philosophical, and moral doctrines. Some of these are perfectly reasonable, and this diversity among reasonable doctrines political liberalism sees as the inevitable long-run result of the powers of human reason at work within the background of enduring free institutions" (3–4). I acknowledge that Rawls's *reasonableness* is not identical with my *entitlement*. But in the course of his discussion it becomes clear, so I judge, that if "reasonable" in the above passage is interpreted as *entitled*, Rawls would happily affirm that too.

We seem stymied. A number of the distinct perspectives on reality and the good life present in our society are 'rational,' 'reasonable'; the people who embrace them are entitled to do so. The test of entitlement does not single out any one member from the totality. But neither is there any other feature, possessed by only one among the totality of comprehensive perspectives, which would justify us in granting to the perspective possessing that feature hegemony in political decision and discussion. That is Rawls's unspoken assumption. What then can function as the basis of decision and discussion on political matters?

The answer Rawls offers is, if nothing else, provocative. Though he himself does not use the term "*consensus populi*," his suggestion, at bottom, is that, in a liberal democracy, the *consensus populi* ought to be used to form the political basis of the discussions and decisions of the citizens. The situation of Locke, in the late seventeenth century, with respect to liberal democracy, was that of having to argue for the institution of this form of political organiza-tion. We, now, are in the fortunate situation of living within estab-lished liberal democracies, some of them now several centuries old.

For any political structure that is not merely imposed on a pop-ulace, there is a shared political culture that undergirds that struc-ture. The subjects understand themselves and their relationships in a certain way, and that communal self-understanding comes to ex-pression in the political structure—with all due allowance for dis-torting factors. So too with liberal democracy. There is a political culture of which the political structure is an expression. Specifically, citizens of liberal democracies understand themselves as free and equal; they take themselves to be—they regard themselves as being—free and equal.

At this point our political theorists are to enter the picture. Let the political theorists among us analyze the political culture—the political 'mind'—of our liberal democracies, with the aim of identi-fying the fundamental organizing ideas of that culture. To say that the citizens of such societies regard themselves as free and equal is an important first stab at that analysis, but it is much too general, much too ambiguous, much too vague. What we need is a much more careful and detailed analysis. That done, let our theorists then "elaborate" or "unfold" (27) those ideas into principles of justice— principles "specifying the fair terms of social cooperation between citizens regarded as free and equal" (4).

It goes almost without saying that the identification by our the-orists of the constituent ideas of our political culture, and the elabo-ration of those ideas into principles of justice, must not be whimsical, arbitrary, or ideological. The principles that our theorists arrive at must be ones that it is reasonable for them to expect all citizens of liberal democracies to endorse *who use the light of our com-mon human reason*. The principles must "win [their] support by ad-dressing each citizen's reason" (143). In due course we will see why Rawls thinks that this is the appropriate stipulation to place on the analysis and elaboration.

It is the principles of justice thus arrived at that are to function as the *basis* of decisions and discussions on political matters. The independent source that Rawls proposes is that two-stage procedure, performed by our theorists, of analyzing the political culture of one's liberal democracy into its constituent ideas, and then elaborating those ideas into principles specifying the fair terms of social cooperation between citizens regarded as free and equal. The principles that are to function as the political basis in our liberal democracy are to be extracted from the shared political culture of that liberal democracy.

Notice, says Rawls, that the principles of justice thus arrived at will be "freestanding" (10) with respect to all the comprehensive perspectives present in society. They will not have been derived from any one of those perspectives—not even from the overlap among them. They will have been derived instead from the shared political culture of the society.

However, if the society is to be at all stable and enduring, the comprehensive perspectives present within the society—or at least the reasonable ones among them—must each find the proposed principles of justice acceptable from its own standpoint.[7] Citizens must "within their comprehensive doctrines regard the political conception of justice as true, or as reasonable, whatever their view allows" (151). "Thus, political liberalism looks for a political conception of justice that we hope can gain the support of an overlapping consensus of reasonable religious, philosophical, and moral doctrines in a society regulated by it" (10). Given that in a liberal democracy no one comprehensive perspective is to enjoy a hegemony that stifles opposition by coercion and persuasion, such an "overlapping consensus" is necessary for the stability and endurance of the society. Yet the source of the principles that are to function as the political basis is independent of one and all comprehensive doctrines. The principles are to be *arrived at*—to repeat—by theoretical reflection on the shared political culture of one's liberal democracy.

And why does the role of citizen in a liberal democracy incorporate the requirement that we base our political decisions and discussions on the yield of the *consensus populi*, rather than on our own religious and philosophical perspectives? Rawls freely acknowledges that there is something paradoxical about the liberal restraint on the use of religious reasons. Speaking on behalf of the objector, he asks:

> why should citizens in discussing and voting on the most funda-
> mental political questions honor the limits of public reason? How
> can it be either reasonable or rational, when basic matters are at
> stake, for citizens to appeal only to a public conception of justice
> and not to the whole truth as they see it? Surely, the most funda-
> mental questions should be settled by appealing to the most im-
> portant truths, yet these may far transcend public reason! (216)

No doubt the liberal position is paradoxical for the reason Rawls cites. It is even more paradoxical for another reason. This is a point I made earlier: given that it is of the very essence of liberal democracy that citizens enjoy equal freedom in law to live out their lives as they see fit, how can it be compatible with liberal democracy for its citizens to be *morally restrained* from deciding and discussing political issues as they see fit?

The novelty of Rawls's strategy is that just as those principles of justice which are to serve as the political basis are to be extracted from the *consensus populi* of one's liberal democracy, so too the rationale for the restraint is to be extracted from that same *consensus populi*. Let me first state what I take to be the core idea; and then introduce the details.

The core idea is this: in a liberal democracy, "political power, which is always coercive power, is the power of the public, that is, of free and equal citizens as a collective body" (216). Citizens in a liberal democracy are free and equal co-holders of political voice. Now suppose that I form my opinion concerning some proposed policy, law, or constitutional provision, on the basis of reasons that I know you do not accept, and conduct my discussion with you on the same basis. In acting thus, I am not giving your view on the matter equal weight with mine; I am not treating your voice as equal to mine. Were I to give your view equal weight with my own, I would not plunge ahead and decide and debate as I do—namely, on grounds that I know you do not accept.[8]

Now for the details. This is what Rawls says by way of rationale for his proposal:

when may citizens by their vote properly exercise their coercive political power over one another when fundamental questions are at stake? Or in the light of what principles and ideals must we exercise that power if our doing so is to be justifiable to others as free and equal? To this question political liberalism replies: our exercise of political power is proper and hence justifiable only when it is exercised in accordance with a constitution the essentials of which all citizens may reasonably be expected to endorse in the light of principles and ideals acceptable to them as reasonable and rational. This is the liberal principle of legitimacy. And since the exercise of political power itself must be legitimate, the ideal of citizenship imposes a moral, not a legal, duty—the duty of civility—to be able to explain to one another on those fundamental questions how the principles and policies they advocate and vote for can be supported by the political values of public reason. This duty also involves a willingness to listen to others and a fairmindedness in deciding when accomodations to their views should reasonably be made. (217)

The thought, I take it, is this: it would be absurd to require of us that we never choose or advocate a policy unless everybody agrees with us on that policy. Rather, it is the *reasons* for our decisions and advocacies that we must attend to, not the policies chosen and advocated on the basis of those reasons. As to those reasons, it would again be asking too much to require that we use only those reasons that everybody *in fact* accepts, or only those that we know everybody accepts. It is asking too much in two distinct respects. In the first place, all that can be required is that we confine ourselves to reasons *that it is reasonable of us to believe* would be generally accepted. *Would* be accepted, *if* what? If those reasons were presented to our fellow citizens, presumably. And second, it cannot be *all one's fellow citizens* whose acceptance is critical. There will be some among them who are not reasonable on the issue in question and some whose views on the issue are not rational. If it were the requirement that one must only use reasons that it is reasonable for one to believe that *everybody* would accept—the unreasonable people along with the reasonable, those whose view on the matter is not rational as well as those whose is—the requirement would seldom if ever be satisfied.

In short, the reasons that one must use in deciding and discuss-

ing political issues are reasons about which it is reasonable for one
to believe that they would be accepted by all those of one's fellow
citizens who are reasonable on the issue, and whose thought about
the matter is rational. One may know that a number of one's reasonable and rational fellow citizens draw different conclusions from
those reasons; that is to be expected. But at least all of us are now
deciding and discussing on the same shared basis.[9]

One final detail. Citizens need not, of course, always undertake
to explain in public why they decide as they do. The requirement,
in that regard, is that they "be able to explain" (217, 243); and not
only able, but "ready" (218, 226).

Let us pull things together by having before us another statement by Rawls of the rationale. Democracy, he says,

> implies . . . an equal share in the coercive political power that
> citizens exercise over one another by voting and in other ways.
> As reasonable and rational, and knowing that they affirm a diver-
> sity of reasonable religious and philosophical doctrines, they
> should be ready to explain the basis of their actions to one an-
> other in terms each could reasonably expect that others might
> endorse as consistent with their freedom and equality. Trying to
> meet this condition is one of the tests that this ideal of democratic
> politics asks of us. Understanding how to conduct oneself as a
> democratic citizen includes understanding an ideal of public rea-
> son. (217–8)

Rawls's Attempt to Identify the Independent Source

Let me begin my critique of Rawls's theory with some comments about his attempt to identify an independent source of principles of justice, to be used as the basis of political decisions and
discussions. Here a considerable number of substantial difficulties
arise. Let us remind ourselves that Rawls's aim at this point is to find
a source that will yield principles of justice which it is reasonable to
expect all one's reasonable and rational fellow citizens to share. The
source Rawls proposes is itself something shared—not those principles themselves, but the shared political culture of an extant liberal
democracy.

Rawls assumes that the *shared political culture* of certain extant societies is what I have been calling *the Idea of liberal democracy*. I see no reason whatsoever to suppose that that assumption is true. Earlier I made the point that no actual society is anything more than *more or less* a liberal democracy in its political structure; the counterpart point here is that no actual society has a political mentality which is anything more than *more or less* liberal in its constituent ideas. The *actual* political culture of a country such as the United States, for example, is a melange of conflicting ideas. Among those ideas are the various strands that go to make up the Idea of liberal democracy. But those are far from universally embraced. A Tocquevillian *description* of the *actual* political mind—the political 'Idea,' in the Hegelian sense—of American society, would bring to the surface a number of conflicting strands. Current controversies about the rights of practicing homosexuals and about the propriety and legitimacy of prayers in the public schools are illustrative examples. On these particular issues, the Idea of liberal democracy yields clear conclusions: homosexuals should enjoy equal freedom under law to live their lives as they see fit, and state sponsored schools should not include prayers as an official part of the school program. Yet large numbers of Americans see otherwise. They do not accept the Idea of liberal democracy at these points. Rawls works with an extraordinarily idealized picture of the American political mind. One can see why: If the Idea of liberal democracy is not identical with the shared political culture of American society, then the prospect of extracting, from that political culture, principles of justice that are both *shared* and *appropriate to a liberal democracy,* is hopeless.

"We start," says Rawls, "by looking to the public culture itself as the shared fund of implicitly recognized basic ideas and principles. We hope to formulate these ideas and principles clearly enough to be combined into a political conception of justice congenial to our most firmly held convictions. We express this by saying that a political conception of justice, to be acceptable, must accord with our considered convictions, at all levels of generality, or in what I have called elsewhere 'reflective equilibrium' " (8). I submit that only if we look at the political culture of American society through the rose-tinted glasses of the Idea of liberal democracy, viewing inconsistencies with that Idea as mere 'deviations' from the regnant 'mind,' will we fail to see that on many issues a good many Americans are firmly opposed to the Idea of liberal democracy. The Idea of liberal democracy does not capture their "considered convictions."

But suppose it were the case that the totality of the fundamental ideas constituting the political culture of American society was identical with the Idea of liberal democracy. The work that Rawls assigns to political theorists raises additional problems with his theory. Our political theorists are to analyze our political mentality into its constituent ideas; that done, they are then to elaborate those ideas into principles of justice. These principles are to be ones that one can reasonably expect the reasonable and rational among one's fellow citizens to embrace. To arrive at such principles is the goal of the task assigned to our theorists.

It would take a good deal of exegetic industry to figure out what Rawls means by "reasonable," and even more to figure out what he means by "rational." In spite of the fact that epistemological concepts and claims are at the very center of his theory, his inarticulateness on matters of epistemology, when contrasted with Locke, for example, is striking.

Some phrases lead one to prick up one's ears in suspicion that the Enlightenment understanding of how reason works is still operative. Rawls has, of course, given up the hope that we can arrive at principles of justice by employing something like the Lockean practice. Rather than supposing that we can get at the moral facts themselves by the employment of our generically human hard wiring, he unabashedly starts with a certain tradition: an on-going political culture. He does not attempt to dig beneath that to 'the things themselves.' What he does say, though, is that the principles proposed must "win [their] support by addressing each citizen's reason" (143), and that they must be ones that one can reasonably expect all citizens to endorse *who use the light of our common human reason.* But our common human reason is always a programmed human reason; what we come to believe by the use of our reason (whatever Rawls might have in mind by that) is a function, in part, of what we already believe. And we differ in our beliefs—differ in particular, now, in our comprehensive perspectives.

In short, Rawls is still working with that same picture of the 'understanding' with which Locke worked, before that penultimate deconstructionist chapter of the *Essay*. The idea is that it is possible for our theorists to remove their comprehensive perspectives from their programming, to deposit them in memory, and then, using only the light of our common human reason, to analyze the ideas of our political culture and elaborate those ideas into principles of justice. It is possible for lay persons to do the same when, handed some proposed principles by the theorists, they consider whether to endorse them. Presumably it is that Enlightenment understanding of the workings of our belief-forming dispositions, including, then, our reason, that accounts for the hope, if not confidence, which Rawls has, that our political theorists will be able to accomplish the task set to them: that they will be able, working in the recommended fashion, to arrive at principles of justice that they can reasonably expect their reasonable and rational fellow citizens to endorse.

The truth of the matter seems to me exactly the opposite. No matter what principles of justice a particular political theorist may propose, the reasonable thing for her to expect, given any plausible understanding whatsoever of 'reasonable and rational,' is *not* that all reasonable and rational citizens would accept those principles, but rather that *not all* of them would do so. It would be utterly *unreasonable* for her to expect all of them to accept them. It would be unreasonable of her even to expect all her reasonable and rational fellow theorists to accept them; the contested fate of Rawls's own proposed principles of justice is illustrative.[10] What is reasonable for her to expect is that her proposals will stir up controversy and dissent not only at the point of transition from the academy to general society, but within the academy.

In short, there is no more hope that reasonable and rational citizens will come to agreement, in the way Rawls recommends, on principles of justice, than that they will come to agreement, in the foreseeable future, on some comprehensive philosophical or religious doctrine. It is odd of Rawls to have thought otherwise; he must have been thinking, as I have suggested, that analysis and elaboration of a shared culture is an enterprise that can be insulated against the effects of our perspectival disagreements.

In one interesting passage (226–27), Rawls concedes the point that I have been making. "Keep in mind," he says, "that political liberalism is a *kind* [my italics] of view." Members of the liberal

family differ from each other not only on "the substantive principles" of justice that they propose, but also on "the guidelines of
inquiry" that they propose for arriving at those. What nonetheless
unites them into members of the *liberal* family is, in the first place,
their agreement on "an idea of public reason." Which is to say, their
agreement that our political decisions and discussions are to be based
on principles yielded by what I have called an 'independent source.'
And what unites them, secondly, is that the "substantive principles
of justice . . . are liberal"—that is, appropriate to the agreement
"that citizens share in political power as free and equal." This second
point amounts to an affirmation of the liberal principle of political
legitimacy: for a constitution and laws to be legitimate, they must
express, or if not express, then at least be consistent with, the agreement that citizens share in political power as free and equal.

Rawls then adds that "accepting the idea of public reason and
[the liberal] principle of legitimacy emphatically does not mean . . .
accepting a particular liberal conception of justice down to the last
details of the principles defining its content." In fact, it does not
even mean accepting principles as general as those that Rawls proposes. "The view I have called 'justice as fairness'," says Rawls, "is
but one example of a liberal political conception; its specific content
is not definitive of such a view."

> The point of the ideal of public reason is that citizens are to
> conduct their fundamental discussions within the framework of
> what each regards as a political conception of justice based on
> values that the others can reasonably be expected to endorse and
> each is, in good faith, prepared to defend that conception so
> understood. This means that each of us must have, and be ready
> to explain, a criterion of what principles and guidelines we think
> other citizens (who are also free and equal) may reasonably be
> expected to endorse along with us.

In short, all that is required is that we agree on the idea of public
reason, that we agree on the liberal principle of legitimacy, and that
we each have a criterion, which our fellow citizens find reasonable,
for testing proposed principles of justice against those two non-ne-
gotiable points of agreement.

We may find, says Rawls, "that actually others fail to endorse the principles and guidelines our criterion selects." "That is to be expected," he adds. It is even to be expected that they will not endorse the criterion itself. Though they find it reasonable, they do not endorse it; "many will prefer another criterion." But "we must have such a criterion," says Rawls.

Why is that? Because this requirement

> imposes very considerable discipline on public discussion. Not any value is reasonably said to meet this test, or to be a political value; and not any balance of political values is reasonable. It is inevitable and often desirable that citizens have different views as to the most appropriate political conception [of justice]; for the public political culture is bound to contain different fundamental ideas that can be developed in different ways. An orderly contest between them over time is a reliable way to find which one, if any, is most reasonable.

This is remarkable. Public reason does not have, and does not have to have, any substantive content—any positive principles of justice. The independent source does not, and need not, yield such principles. We can live without them. We do not need, for political life in a liberal democracy, principles endorsed by all reasonable and rational citizens. We do not need such principles for our political decisions and discussions. The debates that take place within a liberal democracy can be about everything political, except for just two things: the liberal principle of legitimacy and the idea of public reason. Those must be taken for granted.

It turns out, then, that the idea of public reason is *an ideal—* Rawls himself calls it that—and may never be anything more. We debate with each other with the goal in mind of discovering principles of justice that are faithful to the liberal principle of legitimacy and that we can reasonably expect all our reasonable and rational fellow citizens to endorse. We may never find them. That is acceptable. We can live with the fact that the independent source that we have identified does not, and may never, actually yield principles of the sort we thought we needed. It may be that at most what it does is eliminate certain principles. And, to repeat the point made earlier, some of the principles eliminated by the Idea of liberal democracy will not be eliminated by the political culture of an actual society such as the United States, for no actual society, in mind and practice, is more than *more or less* a liberal democracy.

Does the Source Yield the Principles Needed?

I have not thus far mentioned the scope of the restraint that Rawls lays on reasons derived from comprehensive religious and philosophical perspectives. That may have led the reader to assume that the restraint holds for *all* political decisions and discussions. Not so. The restraint holds only for *constitutional essentials* and *matters of basic justice*. Or to look at the situation from the other side: it is only for such issues that the citizens of a liberal democracy are obligated to appeal to public reason. Only on such issues, by and large, will assistance be forthcoming from that source. Certainly it is desirable that the yield of public reason be richer than this, but as long as it is not, we will have to be content with this limited utility, while acknowledging that this "is already of enormous importance":

> If a political conception of justice covers the constitutional essentials and matters of basic justice—for the present this is all we aim for—it is already of enormous importance even if it has little to say about many economic and social issues that legislative bodies must regularly consider. To resolve these more particular and detailed issues it is often more reasonable to go beyond the political conception and the values its principles express, and to invoke nonpolitical values that such a view does not include. (230)

Kent Greenawalt, in two important books, *Religious Convictions and Political Choice*,[11] and *Private Consciences and Public Reasons*,[12] has cogently argued that none of the independent sources proposed by those contemporaries who embrace the liberal position is capable of resolving for us some of the most important and contentious political issues that we face today. Worse yet: on some of these issues, those independent sources are simply irrelevant; they have nothing to say. From the above passage (and plenty of others) it is clear that Rawls concedes that many political issues lie beyond the reach of the independent source that he proposes; hence the qualification, "constitutional essentials and matters of basic justice." He appears relatively content with this limitation, quite clearly because he thinks that public reason, whatever its limitations, is capable of dealing with the most important political issues confronting us. Some of the cases that Greenawalt develops shatter that assumption; the thought unavoidably comes to mind that, rather than spending huge quantities of intellectual imagination and energy on developing the liberal position, perhaps we ought to be considering how to deal with the cases not covered. Let me briefly consider just two of the examples that Greenawalt discusses, and then refer the reader to his books for a full treatment of these, and other, examples.

First, the issue of welfare assistance. On this issue we are faced, in our society, with positions along a continuum that goes all the way from those which hold that government should have nothing to do with welfare, limiting its activities to protecting people against force and fraud, to those which hold that the government is responsible for the distribution of social resources. Now suppose one holds the latter, and then adds, thereby honoring the liberal principle of legitimacy, that the government, in carrying out its responsibility, ought to treat all persons as free and equal. It turns out that this allows for a number of significantly distinct distributive formulas. Let me quote Greenawalt:

> Among the most familiar are the Marxist formula, "From each according to his abilities, to each according to his needs," the utilitarian principle of maximizing average or total welfare, and the suggestion of Rawls that distribution should be equal except as inequality will increase goods even for representative members of the least advantaged economic group. In different respects each of these views treats all citizens as equal. For Marx, each's needs count equally; for the utilitarian, each's capacity for happiness (or some surrogate) counts equally in the search for maximum overall welfare; for Rawls, each's entitlement to resources in a fundamental sense is equal and inequalities are allowed only if everyone is made better off. (*Religious Convictions and Political Choice*, 174)

Greenawalt observes that "a choice among these and other distributive approaches will depend on some initial premise about proper notions of human equality and upon complex judgments about human nature and actual or potential social relations" (174). That

seems definitely correct. But consider the notion of human equality.
What these disputes over the appropriate distributive formula reveal
is that though all who embrace the Idea of liberal democracy agree
in the affirmation that citizens are to be treated as free and equal,
there are significantly different understandings of what we are affirming when we affirm that. Analysis of the constituent ideas of
liberal democracy will not *resolve* our disagreement; if it truly is an
analysis, it will *lay bare* our disagreement. If that which is presented
as an analysis resolves the dispute among competing distributive for-
mulae, then it is something more, or other, than an analysis. For
resolution of the disagreement, convictions derived from some-
where else than our shared political culture will have to be utilized.

That was a case in which Rawls's own preferred principles of
justice give definite guidance for the resolution of an important and
contentious political issue; the difficulty was that the mere Idea of
liberal democracy does not enable us to choose between those principles and various competitors. Several of the other issues that
Greenawalt develops are ones to which the Idea of liberal democracy is just irrelevant. I have in mind various issues that hinge crucially on who has 'standing.' One component of the Idea of liberal
democracy is that all persons who come within the jurisdiction of
the state are to be granted equal protection under law. But that does
not tell us who is a person. And one of the crucial issues in our
raging dispute over abortion is whether the fetus is a person. To this
question, the Idea of liberal democracy has nothing at all to contribute. Indeed, it is compatible with the Idea of liberal democracy to
concede that the fetus is not a person and then to go on to argue that
the equal protection under law which the Idea of liberal democracy
accords to persons ought to be accorded to certain non-persons as
well—specifically, human fetuses.

Is It Fair to Ask Everyone to Use the Source?

Those were issues pertaining to the independent source that
Rawls proposes for the principles that are to serve as basis of decisions and discussions on constitutional essentials and matters of basic
justice: Has the source been adequately identified? Does it yield the

principles wanted? A final question concerning the source is this: Is it equitable to ask of everyone that, in deciding and discussing political issues, they refrain from using their comprehensive perspectives, and appeal instead to the yield of the independent source?

In two regards, it seems to me not equitable. One is a point to which I called attention near the beginning of our discussion. It belongs to the *religious convictions* of a good many religious people in our society that *they ought to base* their decisions concerning fundamental issues of justice *on* their religious convictions. They do not view it as an option whether or not to do so. It is their conviction that they ought to strive for wholeness, integrity, integration, in their lives: that they ought to allow the Word of God, the teachings of the Torah, the command and example of Jesus, or whatever, to shape their existence as a whole, including, then, their social and political existence. Their religion is not, for them, about *something other* than their social and political existence; it is *also* about their social and political existence. Accordingly, to require of them that they not base their decisions and discussions concerning political issues on their religion is to infringe, inequitably, on the free exercise of their religion. If they have to make a choice, they will make their decisions about constitutional essentials and matters of basic justice on the basis of their religious convictions and make their decisions on more peripheral matters on other grounds—exactly the opposite of what Rawls lays down in his version of the restraint.

The second inequity is a kind of unfairness that pertains more to practice than theory. Much if not most of the time we will be able to spot religious reasons from a mile away: references to God, to Jesus Christ, to the Torah, to the Christian Bible, to the Koran, are unmistakably religious. Typically, however, comprehensive secular perspectives will go undetected. How am I to tell whether the utilitarianism or the nationalism of the person who argues his case along utilitarian or nationalist lines is or is not part of his comprehensive perspective?

Rawls's Rationale

What remains to consider is the rationale that Rawls offers. The claim is that if I make my decision concerning some political issue for reasons that I know certain of my reasonable and rational fellow citizens do not accept, and if I furthermore explain to them my reasons for my decision, knowing they do not accept them, then I am not treating them as free and equal with myself. In particular, I am not according them equal political voice with myself. Is this true?

Its truth is certainly not self-evident. Start with a few points that, though important, are nonetheless not quite central. In the first place, if my fellow citizen's agreeing or not agreeing with me has *something* to do with my according him equal political voice, then why is not my *conclusion* the relevant thing rather than my *reason*? The assumption seems to be that if I use reasons you do not accept, then you are right in thinking that I am not treating you as my equal; whereas if I hold to a conclusion that you do not accept for reasons that you do accept, then you would not be right in thinking that I am not treating you as my equal. I fail to see it. After all, it is, in the last resort, the *conclusions* people come to that lead them to support whatever laws and policies they do support.

Second, if my using reasons that I know you do not endorse really does constitute my not treating you as equal, then it constitutes that whether or not the issue is constitutional essentials or matters of basic justice. Is my moral failure perhaps the greater, the more important the issue? I fail to see that it is. Given Rawls's concession that public reason does not yield much in the way of generally accepted principles of justice, his rationale for his restraint on religious reasons, if it were cogent, would have the consequence that even those who most firmly embrace the Idea of liberal democracy would regularly and unavoidably be violating one of the fundamental principles of that Idea.

Third, there is something very much like a fallacy of composition in Rawls's reasoning at this point. To see this, let us separate the reasons I have for my acceptance of a certain policy from the reasons that I offer in public for that policy. There is no reason, in general, why these should be the same. Of course, if I say or suggest that my reason was such-and-such, when in fact it was not, that would be dissembling. But there is an eminently honorable reason for discrepancy between the reason one offers in public discussion for a certain policy, and one's own reason for accepting that policy;

namely, one wants to persuade one's discussion partner to accept the policy, and one knows or suspects that different reasons will attract her from those that attracted oneself. Given this fact of honorable discrepancy, it is a good question to which of these two uses of reasons Rawls's rationale ought to be applied. To the latter, I would think. If I can defend a policy I accept with reasons that you find cogent, what difference does it make to you whether those were also for me the determinative reasons?

So suppose it is true that, when conversing with Ryan, I must, to honor his freedom and equality, offer reasons for the policy I accept which I can reasonably expect him to endorse; and suppose it is true, likewise, that, when conversing with Wendy, I must, to honor her freedom and equality, offer reasons for the policy I accept which I can reasonably expect *her* to endorse. It does not follow that the reasons I offer to Ryan must be the same as those I offer to Wendy. To Ryan, I offer reasons that I hope he will find persuasive; to Wendy, I offer reasons that I hope she will find persuasive. Why must they be the same reasons? They need not even be reasons that I accept—let alone reasons that for me personally were determinative. Ad hoc reasons, tailor-made for one's addressee, seem entirely adequate. And if Wendy listens in on my reasoning with Ryan, and Ryan, on my reasoning with Wendy, what difference does that make? In short, one's reasons do not have to be reasons for all comers.

But what about the claim itself? None of these points speaks directly to that. Is it true that if I decide to accept a proposed policy, law, or constitutional provision, on the basis of reasons that I know some of my reasonable and rational fellow citizens do not accept, I am thereby not treating them as free citizens possessing equal political voice with myself? And is it true that if I defend a proposed policy, law, or constitutional provision, on the basis of such reasons, then too I am not treating them as free and equal citizens? Let us state the issue more sharply. Suppose the policy I decide to accept is such that I know there are some reasonable and rational fellow citizens to whom I cannot defend it with reasons that they accept. Am I violating their freedom and equality in making my decision for those reasons?

I think the answer to that question is: Yes, there is a sense of 'freedom and equality' such that I am violating their freedom and equality, *so understood.* Rather than withholding decision on the ground that, of two opinions of equal weight, one says No and the other says Yes, I embrace my own view of the matter. In doing so, I perforce do not treat the opinions as being of equal weight. And notice that it does not matter whether coercion is in view. Whether the issue at hand is a law to be backed up with coercive force, a rule governing cooperation, or a philosophical issue, it makes no difference: If my opinion is Yes and yours is No, and if, rather than abstaining from decision, I embrace the Yes, then I am not treating your opinion as equal to mine.

The question, though, is whether *this* sense of equality is relevant to liberal democracy. It seems to me about as clear as anything can be that it is not relevant. In a democracy, we discuss and debate, with the aim of reaching agreement. We do not just mount the platform to tell our fellow citizens how we see things. We listen and try to persuade. Typically our attempts at persuasion are on an ad hoc basis: offering to Republicans reasons that we think might appeal to them, if we can find such, to Democrats reasons that we think might appeal to them, if we can find such, to Christians reasons that we think might appeal to them, if we can find such, to America-firsters reasons that we think might appeal to them, if we can find such. And so forth. Seldom, even on unimportant issues, do we succeed in reaching consensus, not even among reasonable and rational citizens of these different stripes. But we try.

Then, finally, we vote. It cannot be the case that in voting under these circumstances, we are violating those concepts of freedom and equality that are ingredient in the Idea of liberal democracy, since almost the first thing that happens when societies move toward becoming liberal democracies is that they begin taking votes on various matters and living with the will of the majority—subject to provisos specifying rights of minorities.

The concept of equal voice that is relevant to liberal democracy is that we shall deal with our diverse opinions by establishing fair voting procedures, and then, within that procedure, give everybody's opinion equal weight. Everybody's voice on the matter being voted on is to count as equal with everyone else's. The judges on the U.S. Supreme Court argue and debate with each other, trying to reach consensus. Most of the time they fail; often their failure is not simply a failure to reach consensus on results, but a failure to reach consensus on how the issue should be approached, what line of reasoning should be determinative. Eventually they vote. In that vote, each judge's vote carries equal weight: a paradigm of treating each other as free and equal.

What is striking about our contemporary proponents of the liberal position is that they are still looking for a politics that is the politics of a community with shared perspective. They see that that perspective cannot, in our societies, be a comprehensive perspective; and that that community cannot be a community which is the social embodiment of a comprehensive perspective. So they propose scaling down our expectations. Take a society that is more or less a liberal democracy, and then consider a single aspect of that society, a single dimension: the political. Think of that, if you will, as constituting an *aspectual* community, a *dimensional* community. The perspective which it embodies will be the shared political culture of the society. That perspective will not be comprehensive; all in all, it will be more like a shared perspective on social justice than a shared perspective on the good life in general, and more like a shared perspective on the nature of the political person than a shared perspective on human nature in general. But that limited perspective and that dimensional community will be sufficient for the purposes at hand.

So-called 'communitarians' regularly accuse proponents of the liberal position of being against community. One can see what they are getting at. Nonetheless, this way of putting it seems to me imperceptive of what, at bottom, is going on. The liberal is not willing to live with a politics of multiple communities. He still wants communitarian politics. He is trying to discover, and to form, the relevant community. He thinks we need a shared political basis; he is trying to discover and nourish that basis. For the reasons given, I think that the attempt is hopeless and misguided. We must learn to live with a politics of multiple communities.

What Does Respect Require?

A final point must be about the Rawlsian rationale for restraint on the use of reasons derived from one's comprehensive perspective.

Rawls's argument is that treating a fellow citizen as free and equal requires not using reasons for political decisions and discussions that one could not reasonably expect one's fellow citizens to endorse. Now the person who embraces liberal democracy does not see himself as participating in an arbitrary resolution at this point. To the contrary: he sees our treating each other as free and equal as a way of paying due respect to what we are—to our status. Not to pay respect, in these ways and others, to what we are, is morally wrong. In *Political Liberalism* Rawls does not call much attention to this phenomenon of morally required respect. He does not think he has to. He thinks the citizens of liberal democracies already recognize that they ought to treat each other as free and equal, so he starts with that communal recognition and argues that failure to impose on ourselves the restraint on religious reasons th'at he recommends would be *inconsistent* with that recognition. Nonetheless, he himself does not regard the recognition as free-floating, but as grounded in what one might call 'the morality of respect.'[13]

Up to this point we have followed Rawls in his practice of looking at the giving of reasons derived from one's comprehensive perspective exclusively from the standpoint of the speaker. We have asked whether the speaker, in offering reasons from his own perspective to someone whose perspective is different, is or is not paying due respect to the freedom and equality of the other person. Suppose that we now look at the same phenomenon from the opposite end, from the standpoint of the addressee. Suppose that you offer to me reasons derived from your comprehensive standpoint; and that I, fully persuaded of the moral impropriety of such behavior by the advocates of the liberal position, brush your remarks aside with the comment that in offering me such reasons, you are not paying due respect to my status as free and equal. Only if you offer me reasons derived from the independent source will you be paying me due respect. To offer me such reasons is to demean me; I will not listen.

Such a response would be profoundly disrespectful in its own way. It would pay no respect to your particularity—to you *in* your particularity. It would treat your particularity, and you *in* your particularity, as of no account. Can that be right? Is there not something about the person who embraces, say, the Jewish religion, that I, a

Christian, should honor? Should I not honor her not only as someone who is free and equal, but *as* someone who embraces the Jewish
religion? Is she not worth honoring not only in her similarity to me,
as free and equal, but *in* her particular difference from me—in her
embrace of Judaism?[14] Of course, I mean Judaism to be taken here
as but one example among many. Are persons not often worth honoring *in* their religious particularities, in their national particularities,
in their class particularities, in their gender particularities? Does such
honoring not require that I invite them to tell me how politics looks
from their perspective—and does it not require that I genuinely
listen to what they say? We need a politics that not only honors us
in our similarity as free and equal, but in our particularities. For
our particularities—some of them—are constitutive of who we are,
constitutive of our narrative identities.

In addition: does not the presence of embodied Judaism in our
midst enrich our common life? Cannot the understanding of politics
by those of us who do not embrace Judaism be enriched by Judaism's understanding of politics? But how could such enrichment
ever take place if, in the public square, we do our best to silence all
appeals to our diverse perspectives, regarding the felt need to appeal
to them here and there as simply a lamentable deficiency in the
scope and power of public reason—a deficiency whose overcoming
we hope for?

No Restraint on Religious Reasons

We have looked at the most influential of the traditional liberal
positions and at the most influential of the contemporary. In both
cases, we have found that the rationale offered for restraint on the
use of religious reasons in deciding and discussing political issues was
far from persuasive and that the proposal made for an independent
source was seriously deficient. Our attention was focused on the
heart of the matter, not on fine-mesh details of rationales and proposals. Had the latter been the case, the proponent of the liberal
position might reasonably have hoped to repair the damage. In fact,
I see no way of doing so. The liberal position looks hopeless. I see
no reason to suppose that the ethic of the citizen in a liberal democ-

racy includes a restraint on the use of religious reasons in deciding
and discussing political issues. Let citizens use whatever reasons they
find appropriate—including, then, religious reasons.

Recently a group of Christians, organized as the Christian Environment Council, appeared in Washington, D.C. Addressing the
national media and the congressional leadership, they spoke up in
support of endangered species, declaring themselves opposed to
"any Congressional action that would weaken, hamper, reduce or
end the protection, recovery, and preservation of God's creatures,
including their habitats, especially as accomplished under the Endangered Species Act." The heart of the reason they offered was
that "according to the Scriptures, the earth is the Lord's and all that
dwells within it (Psalm 24:12), and the Lord shows concern for
every creature (Matthew 6:26)." I fail to see that those Christians,
in offering, in the public square, those reasons for their position,
were violating the ethic of the citizen in a liberal democracy. Let it
be added that if they want to persuade those who do not accept the
Hebrew or Christian Bible as authoritative, they will of course have
to find and offer other, additional reasons for their position.
Whether or not a reason for a position is *appropriate* depends not
only on the position but on one's purpose. Reasons are used for
doing different things.

When I say, "Let citizens use whatever reasons they find appropriate," I do not by any means want to be understood as implying
that no restraints whatsoever are appropriate on a person's reasoning
from his or her religion. Restraints of three sorts pertain to the citizen of a liberal democracy.

In the first place, restraints are needed on the *manner* of discussion and debate in the public square. In our manner of argumentation, we ought to show respect for the other person. Our discussions
ought to be conducted with *civility*. The virtues of civility belong to
the ethic of the citizen.

There will be disputes as to what those virtues are. What does
respect for the freedom and equality of the other person require by
way of *manner* of discussion and debate? What does respect for that
which is of worth in the particularity of the other person require?
My own view is that those virtues prove considerably thicker than
the word 'civility' would naturally suggest. They require *listening* to

the other person with a willingness to learn and to let one's mind be changed. In some cases they require repentance and forgiveness.

Second, the debates, except for extreme circumstances, are to be conducted and resolved in accord with the rules provided by the laws of the land and the provisions of the Constitution. It is certainly not out of place to argue for changes in those laws and in those provisions, but, except for extreme circumstances, that argumentation is itself to be conducted in accord with the extant laws and provisions.

Third, there is a restraint on the overall goal of the debates and discussions. The goal is political justice, not the achievement of one's own interests. Here I side with the liberal position, against the competition-of-interests position.

On what basis do I claim that these restraints belong to the ethic of the citizen in a liberal democracy? Are they grounded in the Idea of liberal democracy? Can they, accordingly, somehow be extracted from that Idea? Not without controversy. The view that the proper goal of political discourse is satisfaction of interests is seen by some as just as compatible with the Idea of liberal democracy as the view of the liberal position, which says that the proper goal is political justice; so too, the view I espouse, that political discourse at its best is governed, among other things, by respect for certain of the peculiarities of one's fellow citizens, is seen by me and others as just as compatible with the Idea of liberal democracy as the view of the liberal position, which holds that it is governed only by respect for the freedom and equality of citizens.

In short: in some measure, at least, it is my own moral and religious perspective that leads me to articulate the ethic of the citizen in a *liberal* democracy as I do. Even at this point of articulating the ethical component of the role of citizen, we cannot leap out of our perspectives. And even if we could, there is nothing firm that we could leap on to: no adequate independent source. The ethic of the citizen is itself up for debate in constitutional democracies of a by and large liberal character.

Do We Need Consensus?

The question that arises at this point is this: do we not *need* what the representatives of the liberal position call a *political basis*?

Do we not *need* an abiding set of agreed-on principles to which all of us, from day to day and year to year, can appeal in deciding and discussing political issues—at least the most important among them, those that deal with "constitutional essentials and matters of basis justice"?[15]

Apparently not. None of our contemporary defenders of the liberal position believes that any extant society actually has such a basis. I think they are right on that. They see themselves not as describing the basis some society already has, but as offering proposals for obtaining such a basis. They think liberal democracies *should have* such a basis; often they speak of such societies as *needing* such a basis. Yet many of our contemporary societies manage to be ongoing constitutional democracies of a relatively liberal character. Apparently, such a basis is not necessary.

We aim at agreement in our discussions with each other. But we do not for the most part aim at achieving agreement concerning a political basis; rather, we aim at agreement concerning the particular policy, law, or constitutional provision under consideration. Our agreement on some policy need not be based on some set of principles *agreed on* by all present and future citizens and *rich enough* to settle all important political issues. Sufficient if each citizen, for his or her own reasons, agrees on the policy today and tomorrow—not for all time. It need not even be the case that each and every citizen agrees to the policy. Sufficient if the agreement be the fairly gained and fairly executed agreement of the majority.

That is the nature of political decision and discussion in constitutional democracies that are relatively liberal in character and whose citizens embody a diversity of comprehensive perspectives: ad hoc, full of compromise, tolerant of losing the vote, focused on the specific, and on the here and now and the near future. Something so jerry-built may not long endure. But the risk is worth taking, and not only because the alternatives are all worse. There is something about each of us that merits respect by each treating each as free and equal.

The Consocial Position

Early in my discussion, I called the position I would be defending the *consocial* position. The consocial position agrees with the liberal position and opposes the competition-of-interests position concerning the goal of political discussions, decisions, and actions: the goal is political justice. But it departs from the liberal position on two defining issues. First, it repudiates the quest for an independent source and imposes no moral restraint on the use of religious reasons. And second, it interprets the neutrality requirement, that the state be neutral with respect to the religious and other comprehensive perspectives present in society, as requiring *impartiality* rather than *separation*. What unites these two themes is that, at both points, the person embracing the consocial position wishes to grant citizens, no matter what their religion or irreligion, as much liberty as possible to live out their lives as they see fit. On the two issues mentioned, he sees the person embracing the liberal position as recommending policies incompatible with the Idea of liberal democracy. We have already noted how the liberal position's recommendation of restraint on religious reasons infringes on the free exercise of religion. Let me now briefly call attention to how the liberal's embrace of the separation interpretation does the same.

The state, in all contemporary constitutional democracies, funds a large part of the educational system. One can imagine a constitutional democracy in which that is not the case; in the contemporary world, however, it always is the case. Given such state funding, the separation interpretation specifies that the state must not in any significant way aid any religion—nor any comprehensive non-religious perspective.

Now suppose there are parents present in society for whom it is a matter of religious conviction that their children receive a religiously integrated education—of a particular sort. Such parents are in fact present in contemporary American society. Were the state to fund an educational program in accord with the religious convictions of any of those parents, it would, obviously, be aiding their religion and thereby violating the separation principle. But conversely, if the state funds other schools but refuses to fund schools satisfactory to those parents who want a religiously integrated education (of a particular sort) for their children, then those parents, in a perfectly obvious way, are discriminated against. If those parents are forbidden by law to establish and patronize schools that teach in accord with their religious convictions, then the discrimination is embodied in law. If they are not legally forbidden to establish and patronize such schools, then the discrimination is embodied in economics. Were those parents to establish and patronize schools that teach in accord with their convictions, they would have to pay for those schools out of their own pockets, while still contributing to the general tax fund for the other schools. Obviously the free exercise of their religion is thereby infringed on—in a way in which that of others is not. They do not enjoy equal freedom, in this regard, to live out their lives as they see fit.

The situation poses an inescapable dilemma for the separation interpretation. Given that interpretation, there is nothing that can be done that does not either violate the separation principle or inequitably infringe on the free exercise of someone's religion or irreligion. The only escape from the dilemma is to give up the separation interpretation and adopt the impartiality interpretation: let the state fund equitably all schools that meet minimum educational requirements.

There is a common pattern to the impression of the person who embraces the liberal position that his insistence on an independent source deals fairly with religion, and to his impression that his insistence on the separation interpretation deals fairly with religion. The common pattern is this: the liberal assumes that requiring religious people to debate and act politically for reasons other than religious reasons is not in violation of their *religious* convictions; likewise he assumes that an educational program that makes no reference to religion is not in violation of any parent's *religious* convictions. He assumes, in other words, that though religious people may not be in the *habit* of dividing their lives into a religious component and a non-religious component, and though some might not be *happy* doing so, nonetheless, their doing so would in no case be in violation of their religion. But he is wrong about this. It is when we bring into the picture people for whom it is a matter of religious conviction that they ought to strive for a religiously integrated existence—then especially, though not only then, does the unfairness of the liberal position to religion come to light.

Application to Public Officials

My attention has been focused on the ethic of the citizen in a liberal democracy, that is, on the ethical requirements embedded in the *role* of citizen: does that ethic include a restraint on the use of religious reasons for political decisions and discussions? Let me conclude with some brief comments on the use of religious reasons by officials: legislators, executives, and judges.

Legislators lie on one side of a divide that is important for this question, and executives and judges, on the other. That divide is this: legislators play a pivotal role in the normal process whereby a democratic society reaches its decisions about the laws that shall govern the interactions of its citizens; executives and judges exercise their roles after the society has reached its decision.

The executive is handed the laws and constitutional provisions, with instructions to administer their implementation and enforcement; the judge is likewise handed the laws and constitutional provisions, with instructions to adjudicate disputes in the light of them. Both are acting on behalf of the community, implementing the community's will. The community has chosen its laws and constitution; now it commissions executives to administer and enforce the law, and judges to adjudicate by reference to the law. Accordingly, when people are functioning in the role of executive or judge, the question of whether they personally approve the laws and provisions never arises; a person is never asked, when functioning in either of those roles, for his personal opinion on the matter. Thus also the question of offering reasons from his religion for or against the legislation or constitution never arises. The role of executive is only to administer and enforce, of judge, to adjudicate. If anyone in the role has moral or religious scruples against doing so, then, depending on how serious the scruples, he or she must get out of the role.

Administration and adjudication are not mechanical procedures; both activities require interpretation. And beyond a doubt the comprehensive perspectives, be they religious or otherwise, of executives and judges, play a role in the processes through which executives and judges arrive at interpretations; it could not be otherwise. Nonetheless the fact remains that both executives and judges are acting on behalf of the community: the community has made up its mind on the law and now wants that law administered, enforced, and used in adjudication. Musical performance also incorporates interpretation. But the musical performer is not interpreting on behalf of anyone. It is open to her to give a totally astonishing, unexpected, even whimsical, interpretation. If she is not thereby irresponsibly shattering expectations, what difference does it make? Not so for executives and judges: they have been duly commissioned to administer and adjudicate, and therefore to interpret, on behalf of the community. Thus the question arises: which interpretations, in the light of which perspectives, are permissible?

The answer in a democratic society is that the citizens themselves eventually answer that question—on the basis of whatever reasons individual citizens find cogent. In effect society says to its executives and judges: go ahead, interpret; we will eventually tell you, by elections, recalls, referenda, protest movements, and so forth, whether we think you have strayed from what is permissible.

The role of the legislator is different. Laws, as he deals with them, are still prospective. Accordingly, reasons for and against their enactment are very much in the picture. The question definitely does arise for the legislator: is it acceptable to make his decision, and then to argue the case, on personal religious grounds?

Though not commissioned to implement society's decision, playing a crucial role, instead, in society's arriving at its decision, the legislator is nonetheless also not a private citizen. He is a representative. But what is it to be a representative? Is it to do what he can to discover the will of the majority of his constituents—or the most powerful among them, or the most vocal—and then vote accordingly? Or is it to decide as he personally judges best—taking into account, as he makes his decision, whatever considerations his constituents may call to his attention? The issue has never been resolved in our societies; some of us hold one view; some, another. On the former construal of the role of representative, whatever reasons the person who is representative may personally have, religious or not, for or against the proposed legislation, do not enter the picture. On the latter construal, they very well may. Indeed, on the latter construal of the role of representative, no general restraint on the use of religious reasons seems relevant or appropriate. The representative must decide as she judges best—after gleaning what wisdom she can from her constituents, and anyone else. Her decision will have to be in the light of all that she believes, including her religion or irreligion, as the case may be. She runs the risk of being removed from office next time around. But that is the risk any representative takes

who sees her role not as one who follows political polls but as one
who exercises political wisdom.[16]

Notes

1. I have in mind here chapter 1 of Jean Cohen and Andrew Arato, *Civil Society and Political Theory* (Cambridge: MIT Press, 1992), which manages to analyze the resistance movement in East Germany of the late 1980s without mentioning that churches and pastors were involved!

2. I will reserve my reflections on the views of my discussion partner, Robert Audi, for my rejoinder.

3. The matters that follow are discussed much more fully in my recent book, *John Locke and the Ethics of Belief* (Cambridge: Cambridge University Press, 1996).

4. I might add that I have developed a much more extended critique in my *John Locke and the Ethics of Belief*.

5. See especially the essays in A. Plantinga and N. Wolterstorff, *Faith and Rationality* (Notre Dame: University of Notre Dame Press, 1982).

6. New York: Columbia University Press, 1993.

7. The qualification, that the principles of justice must be acceptable to the *reasonable* perspectives, if the society is to be stable and enduring, is understandable but nonetheless questionable. By and large it is the *unreasonable* perspectives that constitute a threat to liberal democracies!

8. In an unpublished essay, Paul Weithman treats Rawls's thought as a species of what he calls "the liberalism of reasoned respect," and traces this liberalism to Kant's notion of respect for each other as rational agents. Certainly he is right to see Rawls as working in the Kantian tradition. But I read Rawls, in *Political Liberalism*, as not only more epistemologically chaste than Locke, but also as more epistemologically chaste than Kant. He wants to avoid appealing to any independent notion of *respect for rational agency*. His argument is that the Idea of liberal democracy itself *implies* restraint on the use of reasons derived from comprehensive religious or philosophical perspectives. The notion of *respect*, though it no doubt underlies Rawls's thought, plays no role in the argument itself.

9. Of course, something has to be said about *the reasoning* as well as about *the reasons*, lest thoroughly exotic, and even offensive, conclusions be drawn from eminently acceptable reasons. This is what Rawls says: "on matters of constitutional essentials and basic justice, the basic structure and its public policies are to be justifiable to all citizens, as the principle of political legitimacy requires. We add to this that in making these justifications we are to appeal only to presently accepted general beliefs and forms of reasoning found in common sense, and the methods and conclusions of science when these are not controversial. The liberal principle of legitimacy makes this the most appropriate, if not the only, way to specify the guidelines of public inquiry. What other guidelines and criteria have we for this case?" (224)

10. For those unfamiliar with Rawls's thought on this point, those principles are these two:

a. Each person has an equal claim to a fully adequate scheme of equal basic rights and liberties, which scheme is compatible with the same scheme for all; and in this scheme the equal political liberties, and only those liberties, are to be guaranteed their fair value.

b. Social and economic inequalities are to satisfy two conditions: first, they are to be attached to positions and offices open to all under conditions of fair equality of opportunity, and second, they are to be to the greatest benefit of the least advantaged members of society (5–6).

11. New York: Oxford University Press, 1988.

12. New York: Oxford University Press, 1995.

13. See Rawls, op.cit., p. 19: "The basic idea is that in virtue of their two moral powers (a capacity for a sense of justice and for a conception of the good) and the powers of reason (of judgment, thought, and inference connected with these powers), persons are free. Their having these powers to the requisite minimum degree to be fully cooperating members of society makes persons equal."

14. I am thinking here of Charles Taylor's defense of what he calls "the politics of recognition." See "The Politics of Recognition" in the collection of his essays, *Philosophical Arguments* (Cambridge: Harvard University Press, 1995).

15. An excellent discussion of this issue, far more expansive than I can introduce here, is to be found in Nicholas Rescher, *Pluralism* (Oxford: Clarendon Press, 1993), especially chapter 9.

16. Over a good many years I have benefitted from talking with so many people about the issues raised in the discussion above that it would be unwise now to single any one out. But acknowledgment of my most recent discussions cannot be passed by. First, I am much indebted to those who participated in the conference on "Religion and Liberalism" held at the University of Notre Dame in February, 1996—and especially to Paul Weithman, organizer of the conference. Second, I have very much profited from the incisive, perceptive, and challenging comments of my dialogue partner in this present enterprise, Robert Audi.

WOLTERSTORFF ON RELIGION, POLITICS, AND THE LIBERAL STATE

Robert Audi

Professor Wolterstorff's insightful essay on the role of religion in politics is noteworthy on at least three counts: its portrait of liberal democracy and of liberalism as a theory of how a democratic society should function; its epistemologically informed appraisal of the classical liberalism of Locke and the contemporary liberalism of Rawls; and its forceful presentation of a positive conception of the place of religious conviction in the practice of democratic citizenship. In general the essay is historically informed, epistemologically sophisticated, sensitive to a variety of religious and political perspectives, and judicious in balancing religious and democratic ideals. It is impossible to do it full justice in a study of this scope, and I shall concentrate mainly on the first and third elements just noted: the portrait of liberalism and its relation to democracy and Wolterstorff's own positive view of the place of religious conviction in democratic citizenship. In discussing his essay I shall be especially concerned to bring out contrasts between his views and mine. This should be helpful to the reader but, inevitably, will play down the many important areas of agreement between us.

Liberalism and Religion

There are three aspects of Wolterstorff's account of liberalism that particularly merit discussion in a book on religion and politics: the treatment of the restraints that liberalism tends to impose or at least urge on religious citizens, the rationale for endorsing such restraints, and the kind of neutrality liberalism sees as appropriate to government. I take these in turn.

It is a kind of epistemological restraint that Wolterstorff sees as central in liberalism's restriction of religious considerations in politics. For liberalism, he suggests, it is a requirement of good citizenship "that one's religion not be determinative of one's decisions on political issues, and/or that it not be determinative of the case one makes to others in favor of one's decision" (69). Later he puts the liberal position somewhat differently: "Citizens (and officials) *are not* to base their decisions and/or debates concerning political issues on religious convictions . . . they are to allow their religious convictions to idle" (73). The positive liberal view on this matter is that "They are to base their political decisions, and their political debate in the public space, on the principles yielded by some source *independent of* any and all of the religious perspectives to be found in society" (73), provided it is *fair* to insist that everyone base political decisions on those principles (74).

As to the rationale for endorsing such restraints, Wolterstorff emphasizes two points. The apparently more basic one is that for liberalism "the proper goal of political action in a liberal democratic society, on the part of citizens and officials alike, is *justice*" (73). The second point is that citizens' relying on religious reasons is "just too dangerous," at least in part because "Religion stirs up too many passions" (78).

Regarding the neutrality toward religion that liberalism takes to be incumbent on the state, Wolterstorff notes two interpretations of the idea of restraints on religious reasons as that idea is applied to the state. On the first—the separation interpretation—"government is to do nothing to advance or hinder any religion" (76). On the second—the impartiality interpretation—"government and its agents treat all religions *impartially*" (76). Wolterstorff sees the First Amendment of the United States Constitution—which prohibits government from establishing a religion or abridging the free exercise of religion—as ambiguous between these two interpretations. He sees most liberals as preferring the first, separationist conception of neutrality, but himself prefers the second (which he also takes as consistent with sound constitutional interpretation).

In discussing these three elements in Wolterstorff's portrait of liberalism I shall try to clarify both his position and liberalism itself, especially my own version of it developed in application to the area of religion and politics. To begin with restrictions on religious reasons in the sociopolitical conduct of citizens, I would first note an ambiguity. Recall the claim that, for liberalism, religious reasons must not be "determinative" of one's decisions on political issues (or of one's public case for such decisions). A strong view would require that those reasons not be *a* determining factor at all; a weaker view would simply require that they not be the *only* determining factor; and there are at least as many views along these lines as there are kinds of determination. My position on this matter is quite moderate: I propose that (particularly when advocating or supporting laws or public policies that would restrict liberty) conscientious citizens have a prima facie obligation to have and be willing to offer at least one secular reason that is evidentially adequate and motivationally sufficient (the reason may be compound or otherwise complex and may be constituted by a number of considerations). This allows that one also have, for the law or policy in question, *religious* reasons that are evidentially adequate and motivationally sufficient. Here, then, is one liberal position that provides far more space for the operation of religious reasons than one would expect of liberalism from the characterization of it Wolterstorff gives here.

Indeed, the chief asymmetry in my treatment of secular and religious reasons is in the absence of a counterpart condition regarding religious reasons—one requiring an evidentially adequate and motivationally sufficient religious reason in the same cases. To require this would not only make theological assumptions that are inappropriate to liberalism, but would also require some kind of religious attitude on the part of citizens who conscientiously take part in the full range of democratic decisions open to them as participants in the business of government. Even this asymmetry is compatible with leaving open (as I do) that religious reasons *can* be evidentially adequate for a wide range of sociopolitical conclusions.

If we now consider Wolterstorff's metaphor of *idling* as applied to the liberal conception of the place of religious convictions in politics (73), it is clear that at best it describes highly restrictive versions of liberalism. My view readily accommodates at least the following kinds of mutually compatible sociopolitical work on the part of religious convictions, whether in determining votes and other concrete support of specific actions affecting other citizens, or in determining elements of public discourse. Those convictions may be *genetically basic*, as where the sense of Christian charity initiates and underlies one's desire to help the sick and the poor world wide and leads one to think of good secular arguments for increasing foreign aid. Religious convictions can be *motivationally primary*, as where the sense of Christian charity weighs much more heavily than do secular considerations in sustaining one's efforts to reform foreign policy accordingly; a religious commitment can be motivationally dominant in this way even if a secular sense of obligation is sufficient to produce the same policy stance. Religious considerations can, consistently with my view, be *evidentially adequate*; nothing I say precludes the possibility of there being good grounds of a religious kind for certain principles of conduct, ranging from veracity in human relations—public as well as private—to helping the poor, to obeying the law (here one is reminded of Jesus' famous words, "Render unto to Caesar what is Caesar's" [Luke 20:25]).

Religious considerations can also be *aligned with secular ones* in sociopolitical matters in supporting the same conduct; there is no incompatibility—and in my judgment much reason to expect consistency or even harmony, in both content and implications for action—between good religious reasons for certain laws or public policies and good secular reasons for them. Consider, for example, how many of the ethical Ten Commandments (arguably all of the ethical ones) are supportable both by religious considerations and by any of the leading ethical perspectives, such as Kantianism, utilitarianism (at least in selected versions), intuitionism, and virtue ethics. There is no reason to doubt that a similar harmony can be found in more specifically sociopolitical directives, such as the imperative to aid the poor found in Christianity, Judaism, and Islam. Finally, there is a host of related respects in which various moderate liberal principles—certainly including my principles of secular rationale and motivation—provide for religious convictions' playing important roles in the exercise of citizenship. They may be crucial in expressing one's point of view, in persuading others to join one in a course of action, in enabling one to serve as a role model for people in and outside one's faith, and so forth.[1]

There are many areas in which liberals might seek a rationale for asking citizens to constrain their dependence on religious reasons. Wolterstorff is quite right, however, to emphasize one of them: the importance of justice as a goal of conscientious sociopolitical action in a liberal democracy and the typical liberal fear that religious considerations will arouse passions that ultimately undermine the freedom or democratic harmony of such a society. But unless the notion of justice is stretched enormously, it should not be regarded as *the* only proper goal that liberals take sociopolitical action to have. Even Rawls, who restricts the role of "comprehensive views" in determining the conduct of conscientious citizens, says that the "subject of their [public] reason is the good of the public."[2]

My position on religion and politics does not even rule out reliance on a comprehensive view (though I do not assume everyone has a view deserving of that description) so long as some set of reasons that it provides one for undertaking sociopolitical action is both evidentially adequate and sufficiently motivating for the action in question. To be sure, it may be that in practice the only reasons satisfying this description are of a kind that would belong to an overlapping consensus (as Rawls calls it) among the plausible comprehensive views to be found in a pluralistic democracy. If the reasons are evidentially adequate, they at least *could* properly belong to a wide pluralistic consensus. This question of what restrictions liberalism may properly place on citizens' reliance on their comprehensive views is a difficult issue which—especially in the absence of a clear notion of a comprehensive view—I leave open. My concern has been the special case of religious considerations, regardless of whether (as is the normal case) they belong to a view properly considered comprehensive.

On the matter of passion as a danger of citizens' not constraining their dependence on religious reasons in the ways liberal principles (such as mine) suggest, I heartily agree with Wolterstorff that non-religious issues also arouse passions. I grant, moreover, that arousing passion cannot by itself justify the liberal constraints in question, though I believe he understates the passion that, in political matters, invoking religious considerations tends to arouse. He says that strong passions in American politics "are, for the most part, not attached to such religious reasons as people might have for their political positions, but to those political positions themselves: passionate feelings pro and con about the so-called 'welfare state', for example" (80). One should remember, however, abortion, school prayer, secular humanism, and sex education.

There are, quite beyond the passion issue, many further points of relevance to placing constraints on the reasons we depend on in political decision. A number of these, including the infallible authority often taken to undergird religious considerations, are noted in my essay (31–32). It is the combination of these points that above all seems unique to religious considerations. One should particularly remember that there are religions—including cults—in which some leader is *both* regarded as highly authoritative or even infallible on matters of sociopolitical dimension (such as the permissibility of abortion or homosexual conduct) and influences the voting of citizens, sometimes in ways that can make that voting, if not a case of uncritical obedience, then at least far from autonomous. It can be almost as if many people are magnifying the vote of another rather than exercising their own political will.

Granted, just about anyone's vote may be unduly influenced by other people, but in the case of people unreservedly voting along religious lines there is often a unique potential for undue influence (as in the case of cults). Moreover, that influence may undermine basic liberties, commonly including religious freedom itself, since religious conduct, or its absence, is often and quite appropriately of special interest to religious leaders seeking to guide their constituents in politics. By contrast, secular reasons are not commonly regarded as having the same kind of authority as religious ones, nor are the former in general backed by the same kind of institutional framework of life commitments overseen by revered leaders—a framework in which disobedience is sometimes compelled by mortal threats such as damnation and, when it occurs, often punished by ostracism or worse.

This is a good place to emphasize something easily obscured when we are contrasting religious and secular reasons for sociopolitical conduct. They often support the same positions on law and public policy, especially if we consider religious reasons drawn from the Hebraic-Christian tradition in relation to questions of law and public policy of the kind common in modern Western democracies.

Recall, for instance, the case of charity toward the poor in other nations.

Wolterstorff is apparently much less optimistic about overlap between sociopolitical actions supported by sound secular considerations and such actions supported by the predominant (or at least major) elements in the Hebraic-Christian tradition: "Most people who reasoned from their religion in making up their mind on political issues would lack the intellectual imagination required for reasoning to the same position from premises derived from the independent source. Probably in many cases it just could not be done" (78). I think that if one notes the plethora of secular considerations for and against various political positions in a modern Western democracy, the evidence is against this pessimism. Candidates for office have a track record, a character, proposals, and, generally, advocates and critics. Controversial issues such as abortion, homosexuality, and affirmative action are easily approached from the points of view of natural law and secular justice. Even periods reserved for prayer or meditation in the schools can be defended on the secular grounds of the cultural and ethical values of freedom of religion and reflection.

In addition to differing with Wolterstorff on the likely and extensive alignment between religious and secular reasons, I would ask for examples of cases in which, first, no such overlap can be found and, second, the law or policy in question is supported *only* by religious reasons yet is still one that informed, reflective citizens would wish to defend as appropriate for a religiously and otherwise pluralistic democracy.[3] I am inclined to think that there are few if any such cases.

Concerning the matter of the liberal insistence on the neutrality of the state toward religion, Wolterstorff does well to distinguish the separation from the impartiality interpretations. He does not note, however, that one can treat the separation interpretation as required by the need for neutrality between the religious and the *non*-religious. This neutrality is itself a kind of impartiality. As I argued in my essay (6–8), to promote religion or the religious as such manifests a lack of neutrality regarding those who choose not to be religious. Even beyond this, it is at best difficult for the state to promote religion or the religious without developing criteria for doing so that favor one or another religious group, most likely the majority group if there is one or the most influential group (or coalition of groups) if there is no majority affiliation.

I believe, then, that it is best for the government in a free and democratic society to be not only *neutral among* religions but also *neutral toward* religion.[4] I cannot say too emphatically, however, that this does not require abstaining from adopting policies that have the *effect* of advancing religion. For instance, declaring state holidays when a majority of the people want them for religious reasons will tend to have this effect. But this is not necessarily preference for the religious as such: a government could do the same if a majority felt strongly enough about holidays for economic reasons. More to the point, facilitating the free exercise of religion is a legitimate, if secondary, aim of government under liberalism as I understand it. Doing this is a clear case of a wider aim appropriate to liberalism: helping citizens to do what (within the limits of mutual respect that governments must observe in the legal system) means most to them. A government's doing that is acting for the public good even if it happens that what means the most to the people is religious practice.

To be sure, if facilitating the free exercise of religion is to be entirely consonant with the strictest of the plausible rationales for liberalism, it must not entail a preference for the religious as such. Thus, if there were an aesthetic view of life on which as many citizens centered their lives as in the case of our religions, equal consideration regarding holidays would have to be given to them by a fully liberal regime (they might, for instance, favor summer holidays in order to enjoy that season). Two comments are appropriate here. First, in this case, although the aesthetic view would be *held religiously* (some might call it a "secular religion"[5]), taking account of it in setting holidays would not entail an inappropriate preference. Second, if the view is not so held, then de facto preference for the religious in setting holidays as they wish would be justifiable on the basis of giving priority to promoting liberty and the public good understood (within certain limits) in terms of best satisfying the deepest values of the people, where depth is conceived not in terms of content (here religious content) but of centrality in the lives of the people in question. The religious outlooks would in this second case represent the more deeply held values and would be given preference over the aesthetic values only on that ground.

Wolterstorff's Critique of the Liberalism of Locke and Rawls

Wolterstorff's critique of some main elements in Locke's liberalism seems to me generally sound. Moreover, I am sympathetic with major points in the "Reformed epistemology" he cites as a cogent response to Locke's epistemological position. For Wolterstorff, "Not only is it not the case that one must hold one's religious beliefs for reasons of the Lockean sort to be entitled to them; it is not, in general, necessary that one hold them for any reasons at all. Something about the belief, the person, and the situation, brings it about that the person is entitled to the belief" (87). This view requires two comments in the context of this essay.

First, Wolterstorff does not here elaborate on the kinds of noninferential elements that *do* justify beliefs which are justified other than by "reasons" in the relevant sense, where reasons are, roughly, one or more justificatory premises believed by the person in question. Second, where it seems most plausible to appeal to such noninferential elements as justifying a belief, it is likely to be for beliefs fairly far removed from specific issues of law and public policy. Religious experience, as contrasted with premises, may be plausibly argued to provide justification for accepting the presence of God's love or of God's sustenance of one's life; but if one claims to need no premises for holding that personhood occurs at conception or that foreign aid should be triple what it is, then many deeply religious people as well as skeptics will be doubtful. Nor are these specific claims the kinds generally held by reformed epistemologists to be justified apart from premises.[6]

If, moreover, such specific sociopolitical claims should be regarded as needing no justifying premises, there is the problem of how to prevent *any* religious perspective from claiming equal authority for its non-inferential bases of belief. If justified beliefs of these sorts are agreed to be possible without resting on some adequately supporting premise(s), there are serious problems in denying such justification to myriad conflicting claimants. It is troubling

enough when disagreeing religious groups cite religious premises for
their views: although this helps to make the views intelligible to
others and provides for the possibility of compromise resulting from
discussion of the cogency of the premises in question, it may still
evoke appeals to conflicting world views and authoritative pronouncements by disagreeing clergy. If, however, each side can claim
non-inferential access to (e.g.) divine judgments, the means of
peaceful reconciliation are much reduced.

Both kinds of difficulties are among the problems that lead liberals to argue that secular reasons should be the main basis or an
indispensable part of the basis of conscientious decisions by citizens,
at least in matters that involve coercive laws or public policies. I
believe, then, that although the case for Reformed epistemology
may well suffice (in its most plausible statements) to refute a major
part of Locke's epistemology, the liberal idea that at least for coercive
laws and public policies, adequate secular reasons must be given is
not necessarily brought down with it.

Wolterstorff's extensive treatment of Rawls also deserves discussion (more than I can provide here). In commenting on this
treatment, I am less concerned to bring out the details of Rawls's
multilayered position than to indicate how a liberal position in general can respond to the difficulties that Wolterstorff poses for Rawls.

Early in his treatment of Rawls, Wolterstorff asks how it can be
"compatible with liberal democracy to impose on its citizens a *moral*
restraint on their deciding and discussing political issues as they see
fit" (94). If the moral restraint in question implied a duty so strong
that there is no *moral right* to decide as one sees fit, I would reject
that restraint. But not every prima facie moral duty implies that there
is no right not to perform the relevant deeds, and I have presented
my principles of secular rationale and motivation as expressing an
ethics of citizenship such that although non-compliance may be
morally criticizable, it is not true that in general there is no right not
to comply. One can exercise a right in a reprehensible way.

To be sure, free agents in a liberal democracy do not have an
unrestricted moral right here; there is, for instance, no moral right
to vote on racist grounds. Such injustice is not within our moral
rights, whatever the law may permit. But I do not deny their moral
right to vote on a religious basis. What I maintain (and imagine that

Rawls might also maintain) is that even acting within one's rights may be criticizable from the point of view of good citizenship, morality, or both. Liberalism is committed to protecting freedom even where it is, in any of a variety of ways, ill used; it is not committed to giving up criticism of such ill use.

A related problem that Wolterstorff raises for Rawls is that the latter uncritically holds that "the principles proposed [by a sound liberalism] must 'win [their] support by addressing each citizen's reason', and that they must be ones that one can reasonably expect all citizens to endorse *who use the light of our common human reason*" (98). To this, Wolterstorff replies that our common human reason is "programmed" and that what we come to believe by the use of reason is in part a function of what we already believe. "And we differ in our beliefs—differ in particular, now, in our comprehensive perspectives" (98).

There certainly are problems here, but perhaps they are not insurmountable. First, even if we are all programmed in some sense, the initial programming may come significantly from something universal, such as perception, which may in turn yield a goodly store of our earliest beliefs. These are not, to be sure, based on "reasons," but they and the natural tendencies that their formation reveals may well be part of what Rawls means by "our common reason." Second, different as we are in our beliefs, we share many, and certainly *can* share many if we try to expose ourselves to the same data and to reason together using ordinary techniques of deductive and inductive logic, techniques of a kind that seem virtually universal. This is hard to show; but even if it is an article of liberal faith, it is not refuted by the plausible points Wolterstorff makes here. Let me provide some support for this point by addressing a related criticism of the liberal view, or at least of Rawls's version of it.

Continuing his emphasis on our diversity of outlook, Wolterstorff says that there is "no more hope that reasonable citizens will come to agreement, in the way Rawls recommends, on principles of justice, than that they will come to agreement, in the foreseeable future, on some comprehensive philosophical or religious doctrine" (99). I would think that if we stick to principles of justice, which form only a small part of a comprehensive view, and if we do not take agreement to imply unanimity as opposed to consensus, there is a better chance of agreement than on the whole of such a larger view. Perhaps the chance is still not good, especially if it must be *through* a veil-of-ignorance procedure such as Rawls proposes in *A Theory of Justice*. But is there not a strong consensus, at least among citizens of democratic societies, that justice requires not only equal protection of the laws but also laws that protect liberty, including political and religious liberty and freedom of speech, up to a certain level? There are of course disagreements on matters of detail even among those who hold similar overall standards of justice, say differences over what income-tax rate would be fair. But at least some of these disagreements will disappear if the differing parties can agree on all the relevant facts, such as facts about the economic effects and the different incentives that go with a given rate of taxation.

Whatever differences may persist among rational citizens on principles of justice, it must be emphasized that there is a difference between agreement *on* principles and agreement *in* principles, and there is a related difference between agreement in practice and agreement in underlying intuitions.[7] Let me take these distinctions in turn.

Just as two people can use a term similarly and, indeed, mean essentially the same thing by it, yet offer incompatible accounts of its meaning (providing definitions is a demanding theoretical task), they can disagree on what principles of justice we should hold and still agree in concrete cases that justice has been served or that an injustice has been done. Many different definitions can be applied to the same finite range of cases, and this holds whether we are speaking of justice or of other elusive notions, such as intention or knowledge or explanation. More commonly still, people may agree on the relevant kind of right and wrong actions, such as allowing freedom of speech for two different groups and taxing the rich proportionately less than the poor, even if they do not use the *terms* 'justice' and 'injustice' in describing those actions. This would be a case of broad moral agreement without the same moral diagnosis. For harmonious coexistence, the former is more important than the latter.

The second distinction is subtler. Two people who disagree on the justice of allowing a Nazi group to present its case may share intuitions about free speech in general and be divided by, for instance, paranoia about Nazis, which one party has and the other does not. When this happens, there is often a possible route from the shared intuitions about the justice of protecting freedom of expression to agreement on the case at hand. It appears, moreover, that among rational civilized people, establishing agreement on what factual information is relevant and on what the relevant facts are tends to bring intuitions closer together.

None of these points is meant to underplay the importance of deep disagreements among citizens or the possibility that some of those disagreements are ineliminable. I simply want to show that some disagreements may not be as deep as they look and that others can be eliminated under certain conditions of communication, careful reflection, and shared factual information. Having said this, however, I want to stress that liberalism is not committed to the possibility that all important sociopolitical disagreements can be resolved. Liberalism is designed not to eliminate all disagreements but to nurture conditions that keep disagreements from tearing apart the fabric of civic life.

Another implication that should not be attributed to liberalism is the idea that a citizen's remaining unmoved by the arguments of others, even the majority, shows disrespect for them. Wolterstorff can easily be read as taking liberalism to have some such commitment when he attributes to Rawls the claim that "if I make my decision concerning some political issue for reasons that I know certain of my reasonable and rational fellow citizens do not accept . . . then I am not treating them as free and equal with myself" (105–6). I agree in rejecting this but do not see Rawls—and certainly not liberalism in general—as committed to it. Let me explain.

Rawls does say that "our exercise of political power is proper and hence justifiable only when it is exercised in accordance with a constitution the essentials of which all citizens may reasonably be expected to endorse in the light of principles and ideals acceptable to them as rational and reasonable" (217) and that citizens "should be ready to explain the basis of their actions to one another in terms each could reasonably expect that others might endorse as consistent with their freedom and equality" (218). But he is here speaking above all about coercive state power in relation to matters of basic justice, not about *every* political issue, such as who is the best candidate for a senate seat or how much foreign aid we should give. Moreover, the emphasis is not on actual agreement, even on "constitutional essentials," but on its realistic *possibility* given rationality and, I suspect, some very basic moral intuitions that are common to mature rational adults who are conscientiously devoted to living together in harmony. As applied to the subject of this book, the implication is that religious reasons will not be acceptable to those with a conflicting religious perspective (or none).

Let us, however, explore whether liberalism in general (as opposed to Rawls's particular version) is committed to the strong conclusion that if one does coerce others on a basis (such as religious conviction) that they cannot be expected to accept (as they can considerations of public safety), one is not treating them as free and equal with oneself. It does seem to me that liberalism is committed to the view that requiring adequate secular reasons for coercive laws and public policies best *accords* with treating citizens as free and equal—these are the kinds of reasons that any rational citizen may be expected to recognize as having at least significant justificatory force. But it does not follow that every case of coercion on a different kind of basis conveys the opposite attitude. Failure to fulfill an ideal does not imply fulfilling an opposite ideal.

At this point, however, it is well to sharpen our focus to the main issue at hand: religious considerations. For any of us who are religious, the prospect that we might be coerced by preferences based on some other religion is generally loathsome. Few have a similar reaction to coercion plausibly imposed for purposes of maintaining law and order or public health or a minimal level of education. Liberalism is in part a response to the intuitive difference nearly everyone feels in such cases. Any plausible theory of the basis of the state that makes the protection of liberty central must do justice to this difference. Liberalism claims to be a common element in such theories.[8]

Wolterstorff is aware that even if one does not imply inequality with oneself by offering to others religious reasons for political positions, one may offend or needlessly alienate them. He thus notes that there is "an eminently honorable reason for discrepancy between the reason one offers in public discussion for a certain policy, and one's own reason for accepting that policy; namely, one wants to persuade one's discussion partner to accept the policy, and one knows or suspects that different reasons will attract her," though "if I say or suggest that my reason was such-and-such, when in fact it was not, that would be dissembling" (106). Why, then, should liberalism ask that in general public political debate be conducted in terms of public reason (or secular reason, for that matter), as opposed to the reasons most likely to persuade the audience in question?

My view on this question is apparently more permissive than Rawls's: I take it to be largely a matter of practical wisdom what reasons to bring to public political debate, though I note that using religious reasons may be highly divisive. But I believe Rawls's position is close to mine in implying (perhaps quite indirectly) that the reasons for which one actually makes political decisions, especially those involving coercion of fellow citizens, should justify those decisions by secular standards. In any case, what I want to address here is Wolterstorff's suggestion that one may honorably offer reasons in public that are not one's real reasons for the position they are offered as supporting. How is one to do this without insincerity or "dissembling"?

One possibility is simply saying such things as "Here are two good reasons for this position," where one takes the reasons to be convincing to one's audience but is not oneself moved by them. A second possibility is pointing out reasons the audience already has, at least implicitly, that support the policy, whether one thinks they are good reasons or not. The first case is troubling: we have to imagine someone thinking a reason for a position to be good, yet not having that as a reason for holding the position. This is extremely rare in rational people, especially if they *hold* the position, which one will if one is sincerely trying to persuade others of it. If I think the reason I give is good, and I hold the position I take it to support, I will normally hold the position—at least in part—for that reason.

The second case, by contrast, is really not one of offering reasons *for the position*; it is offering reasons *for the audience to hold the position*. I would call this *leveraging* by reasons: one tries to move an audience to a view by noting one or more reasons there are for it *from* the audience's point of view.[9] This is compatible with not holding the position and even with thinking that the reasons do not in fact support it.

A third possibility is to offer reasons one thinks will convince one's audience but does not believe good (this need not be leveraging since one may be persuading the audience of a new point of view as opposed to appealing to an antecedent one). I am sure Wolterstorff would not endorse this practice. At best, it manipulates people; it tends to undermine good reasoning in those who are taken in; and it tends to be deceitful as well, since it is very difficult to present reasons for a view in a convincing way without implying that one takes them to support it.

The first and last points seem to me also to apply to presenting *good* reasons that are not one's own: doing this tends to manipulate others—whom one is in effect asking to accept something on a ground that does not move oneself—and certainly a convincing presentation of the reasons will make it appear (contrary to what is the case) that they are one's own.[10] As to leveraging by appealing to reasons the audience already has, consider the typical case in which it is done so as to avoid giving the audience warrant for concluding that one is offering reasons one accepts as genuinely supporting the position in question—as one normally accepts reasons one offers in promoting a position one holds. Here it is likely to be evident that it *is* leveraging; for plainly one is pointing out why, from the audience's point of view, the position is worthy. That may or may not undermine one's effectiveness in persuading.

Leveraging has an important place in political discourse. But if it is all I do, the audience cannot see *who* I am; I am like a lawyer representing a client in court: my job is to represent the client's point of view within certain limits, and my personal view does not matter. This is for the most part not a good way to relate to fellow citizens. It tends to conceal much of my perspective and so does not promote understanding of me or my view; and it tends to arouse suspicion and so is likely either to undermine my efforts at persuasion or to make me seem an unknown quantity whose future conduct may be unpredictable.

There are, then, good grounds for thinking that in the main the reasons one offers for a position in public should be among one's own reasons for holding it. They may of course not be *all* of these;

but if it tends toward insincerity to offer reasons for a position one holds that are not among one's reasons for holding it, it also tends toward insincerity to offer reasons for it that are not (motivationally) sufficient for one's holding it. If one successfully adheres to the principles of secular rationale and secular motivation, one is presenting reasons that are evidentially sufficient and so should tend to be persuasive to a rational audience irrespective of its point of view, and one is being sincere, and so should not arouse the suspicion that easily arises from offering reasons that are not one's own.

These considerations about the importance of sincerity may illuminate an insightful critical comment that Wolterstorff makes about liberalism, notably Rawls's version but not restricted to that: the liberal "is trying to discover, and to form, the relevant community. He thinks we need a shared political basis . . . I think the attempt is hopeless and misguided. We must learn to live with a politics of multiple communities." I agree that it is hopeless for a pluralistic society to operate as a single community in the sense in which that implies a shared overall view of the world, including religious and sociopolitical outlook. But suppose we distinguish first- and second-order communities. Why it is not possible to seek a *second-order community* whose members are the different and overlapping religious, ethnic, professional, and other communities of which Wolterstorff speaks? Members of the second-order community have less in common than those of the first-order ones, but a commitment to liberal (or other) principles of mutual self-government and civic activity can do much to nurture understanding and tolerance.

This is not to deny that a free and democratic society has much to gain from the diverse contributions of its different and sometimes conflicting communities. As Wolterstorff puts it, "Is there not something about the person who embraces, say, the Jewish religion, that I, a Christian, should honor?" (110–11). A liberal conception of the larger community need not preclude people's expressing and even being politically motivated by special features of their religious or sociocultural point of view. Wolterstorff seems doubtful about this and asks "how could such enrichment ever take place, if, in the public square, we do our best to silence all appeals to our diverse perspectives . . ." (111). Even for Rawls (whom he is here implicitly criticizing), there are ways to draw on diverse perspectives in political debate. But on my view, which is less restrictive than Rawls's in this regard, there is no imperative to silence appeals to diverse points of view, including religious ones—freedom of expression is largely unaffected other than by considerations of prudence. It should be added that a point of view, religious or other, can *inform* a stance one takes in public debate even if one does not refer to that point of view or identify it. Christian charity, for instance, can work this way, say in welfare policy or foreign aid.

Speaking more positively, on my view, it is the advocacy and the support of laws and public policies that are constrained, and the constraint is *inclusive* rather than *exclusive*: the chief point is not that one cannot have and be motivated by religious reasons but that one should have and be motivated by at least one set of evidentially adequate secular reasons. Non-religious reasons that are highly personal are also permissible, and may be highly desirable, in the overall mix. The idea is above all both to make room for full individual expression and at the same time to constrain the grounds for coercion in ways that are, or should be, acceptable to all the diverse parties to political debate.

One might think that this constraint goes against the religious convictions of many in our society, those who hold "that *they ought to base* their decisions concerning fundamental issues of justice *on* their religious convictions . . . that they ought to strive for wholeness, integrity, integration, in their lives; that they ought to allow the Word of God, the teachings of the Torah, the command and example of Jesus, or whatever, to shape their existence" (105). This statement of conviction—call it the religious-basis-of-citizenship view—has inclusive, neutral, and exclusive interpretations. On the first, one must have a sufficient religious basis for one's sociopolitical conduct but may also have an (evidentially) independent basis compatible with that, such as a basis in political philosophy. On the second, one must have a sufficient religious basis, and nothing is said about any other (compatible) basis. On the third, one must have *only* a religious basis. Only the third interpretation would prevent a religious person who holds the position from abiding by the secular rationale and motivation principles. But this interpretation is one that a huge proportion of religious people—and probably most educated religious people—would reject.

By contrast, the first two interpretations of the religious-basis-of-citizenship view allow religious people who hold them to concentrate on making their religion central in their lives while endorsing the rationale and motivation principles as general standards for their advocacy or support of coercive laws or public policies. Depending on their theology, they might, more often than would be consonant with civic virtue, have to take their prima facie obligation to have adequate secular reason to be overridden. But if I have been right about the prospects for theo-ethical equilibrium (and perhaps even if I have been overoptimistic about this prospect), this should occur at most on rare occasions.

Wolterstorff's Positive View of Religion and Politics

Much of Wolterstorff's positive view emerges in his extended critique of Locke and Rawls, but the last section of his essay is devoted to stating a number of further essentials of his own view. He recognizes three kinds of restraints on citizens in a liberal democracy. First, political discussions should be conducted with civility; second, "debates, except for extreme circumstances, are to be conducted and resolved in accord with the rules provided by the laws of the land" (113); and third, "the goal [of debates and discussions] is [to be] political justice . . . Here I side with the liberal position, against the competition-of-interests position" (113). Within these limits, "Let citizens use whatever reasons they find appropriate" (112).

I am largely in agreement with the three main points Wolterstorff makes, though I would hasten to add that (as he doubtless realizes) provision must be made for cases in which the laws of the land are seriously defective and do not deserve our allegiance. I believe, however, that his position may well be more liberal than it looks, if we take his third point to be one of agreement with the liberal. In stating that point it appears that Wolterstorff is acknowledging a conception of political justice that citizens can appropriately rely on independently of its endorsement by a religious view. If so, and if political justice is the overarching goal he takes it to be, then he is quite close to implying that at least our main reasons for sociopolitical decisions (particularly concerning the legal structure of society) should be secular and presumably in some sense public.

This is not in the least to suggest that a rational theist should find anything objectionable in a secular conception of political justice adequate to play the unifying role of providing an overarching aim of sociopolitical conduct. Indeed, if my essay is correct in holding that such a conception should emerge in a theo-ethical equilibrium of the kind expectable on the assumption of God's being omniscient, omnipotent, and omnibenevolent, there should be a theistic route to some at least highly similar conception. The point is that as stated the goal of political justice seems to be independent of religion in the way a liberal conception requires of a goal constitutive of the second-order community comprising a pluralistic liberal democracy.

Since Wolterstorff is criticizing liberalism in this essay, it seems better to read him as intending that citizens belonging to the diverse religious and other groups that compose a free democracy may use their own, often religiously influenced, conceptions of political justice. Take his example, approvingly cited, of the Christian Environmental Council, which has defended endangered species. "The heart of the reason they offered was that 'according to the Scriptures, the earth is the Lord's . . . (Psalm 24:12), and the Lord shows concern for every creature (Matthew 6:26)' " (112). Leaving aside the difficulty of understanding this effort as aimed at "political justice," we can certainly agree that the council's conception of the good of the society in question (or of the world) is religious. Whatever Wolterstorff's conception of political justice, we can at least conclude that he is not restricting citizens to secular goals for political activity.

There are some liberals who would criticize such a use of religious reasons and *exclude* it from proper political conduct in a liberal democracy. On my view, these reasons are not excluded; the main point is to *include* some sufficient secular reason. Plausible candidates are not difficult to find: sentient creatures suffer and flourish and should be preserved so far as possible; the diversity and balance of nature is beautiful; many people deeply *want* a world with all the species we have. I grant that these reasons may not be among the *generative* ones for the council members, but that does not preclude them or other secular reasons from being motivationally *sufficient*.

Suppose, however, that the extent to which secular reasons can be adequately assimilated into one's thinking is not such as to make them sufficiently motivating apart from a sense of divine command to do what they support. I doubt that this would commonly happen, but suppose it did. For my part, I would be at best reluctant to compel non-religious citizens—and disagreeing religious ones—to spend limited tax dollars for a purpose I could not be sufficiently motivated to pursue by secular reasons. If the only reasons that move me are religious, and if I would not want to be coerced on the basis of religious reasons playing a like role in someone with a conflicting religious perspective, I would want to abstain from coercion.

Three points are appropriate here. First, I would still have a right to support such a program. Second, if I have adequate secular reasons for the support—or there exist such, unbeknownst to me, say the necessity of preserving endangered species for maintaining the balance of nature—then no harm should be expected from achieving the purpose. (As this suggests, the principle of secular rationale is more important to the liberal conception of good democratic citizenship than the principle of secular motivation.) Third, this is not a case of coercion of fellow citizens in a matter of basic liberty or having the immense national importance of, say, military conscription in wartime or mandatory prayer sessions in public schools.

Another example that Wolterstorff cites is instructive: the case of state funding for religiously affiliated schools:

> The situation poses an inescapable dilemma for the separation interpretation . . . there is nothing that can be done that does not either violate the separation principle or inequitably infringe on the free exercise of someone's religion or irreligion. The only escape is to . . . adopt the impartiality interpretation: let the state fund equitably all schools which meet minimum educational requirements. (116)

In discussing vouchers in my essay (30), I argued that such a proposal may be consistent with my position. Here I would add that if we take the separation interpretation to prohibit the state's acting *in order to promote* religion and not its acting *in a way that promotes* religion, Wolterstorff's dilemma can be avoided. The state may properly promote an educational system that serves the people's desires provided it is academically adequate and does not have certain adverse effects, such as causing a civil war (and that consideration is not necessarily a church-state issue).

To be sure, there are reasons for the state to avoid entanglement with religion. These, however, do not obviously preclude some kind of voucher system, in part because it would apply to private schools in general and the distinction between those that are religious and those that are not is secondary. But even prohibiting entanglement would not imply prohibiting legislation that would have the *effect* of promoting religion. The effects of legislation go beyond its purposes, and I cannot see that liberalism need require that the state avoid promoting any community by legislation that is otherwise warranted. This applies particularly where the state is in any case bound to protect the freedom of that community and the legislation is justified by this purpose.

When it comes to the delicate matters of administration and adjudication, Wolterstorff again suggests that religious considerations may play a significant role. Here, however, he is not as specific. To the question of which interpretations and perspectives for providing interpretations are permissible, he replies, "The answer in a democratic society is that the citizens themselves eventually answer that question—on the basis of whatever reasons individual citizens find cogent. In effect society says to its executives and judges: go ahead, interpret; we will eventually tell you . . . whether we think you have strayed from what is permissible" (118). This is a very good description of much of what actually occurs in a democracy. But I doubt that Wolterstorff means to suggest that there are no criteria, drawn from religion or ethics, for instance, for proper interpretation. Recall the idea of political justice as the proper goal of the activity of citizens acting as such in a liberal democracy. Or consider some plausible conception of the common good as such a goal. I think, then, that we are back to the question of what sorts of constraints are needed in an ethics of citizenship.

My essay answers this question only in relation to religion and politics. In that domain I have focused on the institutional issues of church-state relations and the individual problems of how to take account of religious considerations in one's conduct as a private citizen. My effort has been to show that, and to some extent how, a liberal democracy should separate church and state institutionally and how individuals should separate religious and secular considerations in their conduct as citizens. But separation need not create a gulf that is never crossed by communication. There need be no unbridgeable gulf either between governmental and religious institutions or between individuals of differing religious positions. Nor need there be a split within individuals who are considering both religious and secular reasons for political conduct.

Cooperation between church and state is possible even if each abstains from unduly influencing the other. Citizens who meet and argue under conditions of mutual respect can draw on both religious and secular considerations in arriving at an understanding even if in the end they hold themselves to having at least one evidentially adequate and motivationally sufficient secular reason for at least those political decisions that are coercive. And religious citizens who seek an equilibrium between their religious commitments and secular grounds for their preferred political actions can benefit from the effort of integration. Quite commonly, they can also enhance both their plausibility to those outside their faith and their motivation to realize the ideals they can most wholeheartedly believe in as citizens of a pluralistic democracy in which they wish to be treated by the same standards of civility and political decision that they themselves embody.

Notes

1. In "The Place of Religious Argument in a Free and Democratic Society," *San Diego Law Review* 30 (1993), I describe a number of the roles in question here.

2. John Rawls, *Political Liberalism* (New York: Columbia University Press, 1993), 213. A few lines later he speaks of "the good of the public and matters of fundamental justice," which confirms that he is not taking fundamental justice to encompass this good.

3. I am speaking here, as Wolterstorff is, of evidentially supporting reasons, not of motivating reasons. There is less likelihood, other things equal, of finding secular reasons that are *both* (especially given how easy it is to find selfish secular reasons that are not evidentially good), though here too I believe that it is easy to be too

pessimistic, particularly where the law or policy in question is one having merits of the kind that make reflective citizens tend to endorse it.

4. Neither kind of neutrality precludes restricting a religious group insofar as its activity is, in a certain way, morally outrageous, as where it practices human sacrifice. This is consistent with neutrality toward the religion as such; the restriction is a consequence of basic governmental protection of its people. Large tax deductions for charitable work could also specially apply to (and benefit) the members of a religious group, but this is not promoting them *as* religious. This issue is explored further in the section on civic virtue and religious conviction, when vouchers for private schools are discussed.

5. John Dewey distinguished among the concepts of religion, *a* religion (a specific realization of religion), and the religious—the notion appealed to in the text—which encompasses the attitudes appropriate to a religion but does not entail the possessors of those attitudes having one. For a historically informed discussion of the notion of "secular religion"—which Dewey might have called a combination of religion and the religious without *a* religion—see Quentin Faulkner, "Religion, Culture, and the Arts," forthcoming in *Soundings*.

6. For a seminal presentation of a Reformed epistemology of religious experience see Alvin Plantinga's "Is Belief In God Properly Basic?" *Nous* 15 (1981): pp. 41–51, and for a wide-ranging epistemology of a similar kind see William P. Alston, *Perceiving God* (Ithaca and London: Cornell University Press, 1991). I have critically appraised the former in "Direct Justification, Evidential Dependence, and Theistic Belief," in *Rationality, Religious, Belief, and Moral Commitment*, eds. Robert Audi and William J. Wainwright (Ithaca and London: Cornell University Press, 1986) and the latter in "Perceptual Experience, Doxastic Practice, and the Rationality of Religious Commitment," *Journal of Philosophical Research* 20 (1995): pp. 1–18.

7. This is similar to a distinction between agreement *on* reasons and agreement *in* reasons that I make in chap. 11 of my *Moral Knowledge and Ethical Character* (forthcoming from Oxford University Press in 1997). Elsewhere in that book, and especially in chap. 2, I argue for the possibility of a high degree of agreement on the kinds of intuitive principles of prima duty that W. D. Ross proposed in *The Right and the Good* (Oxford: Oxford University Press, 1930).

8. Granted, military conscription is deeply objectionable to some, but where the objections are sufficiently deep, liberalism provides for exceptions, typically under the heading of minority rights. A sophisticated coercion by religious considerations might provide for something similar, but historically coercion in the name of religion has not been flexible in that way.

9. Granted, a reason offered in leveraging may *be* in itself a good one, evidentially; but in leveraging one is not offering it as such, but *relative* to the point of view one is in a sense taking. For discussion of leveraging and of the question of the need for sincerity in giving reasons, see my "The Ethics of Advocacy," *Legal Theory* 2, no. 1 (1995): pp. 1–31.

10. I have defended this point in "The Ethics of Advocacy," just cited, and in "The Separation of Church and State," *Philosophy & Public Affairs* 18, no. 3 (1989): pp. 259–96.

AUDI ON RELIGION, POLITICS, AND LIBERAL DEMOCRACY

Nicholas Wolterstorff

Professor Audi's articulation and defense of a version of what I called "the liberal position" stands out from its competitors in several ways. Let me mention two. It is, for one thing, an epistemologically sophisticated defense. In my initial contribution I remarked that all too many contemporary defenders of the liberal position do not model themselves after their great predecessor, John Locke, in the epistemological sophistication that he brought to the discussion. The relevance of this lament on my part is that almost all formulations and defenses of the liberal position make abundant use of epistemological concepts and theses. Robert Audi's articulation of the liberal position, here and elsewhere, is a shining exception to the contemporary generality. Prior to writing on these matters, Audi spent the major portion of his career working and writing on epistemology and moral theory. That shows. Second, Audi's discussion is remarkable for the sympathy for religion that it exhibits and, beyond sympathy, the sophisticated understanding. It is not unusual for contemporary formulations of the liberal position to exhibit a rather primitive understanding of religion—sometimes even, hostility. That is not so for Audi's discussion.

Just above, I spoke of Audi's position as a version of what, in my initial contribution to this discussion, I called "the liberal position." In two respects, that is not quite accurate. In my initial contribution I took the liberal position to include the thesis that "the proper goal of political action in a liberal democratic society, on the part of citizens and officials alike, is *justice*." Audi certainly does not embrace the *self-interest* thesis that I held up as the main alternative:

that the proper goal, on the part of citizens and officials, is maximization of self-interest. But he appears to me also not to embrace what I said those who hold the liberal position embrace as the proper goal. He apparently regards the proper goal as broader than justice—call it, *the social good.*

I now think it was ill-advised on my part not to define the liberal position in the broader way that this suggests—not to define it as incorporating the thesis that the proper goal of political action in a liberal democratic society, on the part of citizens and officials alike, is *the social good or some element thereof.* Any one who embraces the narrower position, that the proper goal is *justice*, will then be espousing a *version* of the liberal position.

There is a second, and more important, way in which Audi's position is not a version of the liberal position, as I defined and explained that. I said that fundamental to the liberal position is the thesis that citizens and officials are *not* to base their decisions concerning (at least fundamental) political issues, nor their discussion of those issues in the public space, on their religious convictions, but are to base them *instead* "on the principles yielded by some source independent of any and all of the religious perspectives to be found in society." Audi does not accept the "not . . . instead" component of this statement. He does hold that citizens and officials must have evidentially adequate and motivationally sufficient reasons independent of their religious convictions for the political positions they take up; but he does not proscribe their having and being motivated by religious reasons *in addition.* His position on the matter is thus inclusivist, rather than exclusivist. I might add that this is another important singularity of his view.

Should I have defined and explained the liberal position in such a way that, in this regard also, Audi's view turns out to be a *version* of the liberal position rather than, as it presently turns out, a close *relative*? It all depends on which of these two ways of classifying views and naming them is the more helpful and illuminating; it is not a matter of getting it right or getting it wrong. (The issue is an interesting example of a new entity or phenomenon forcing one to rethink a classification devised without that entity or phenomenon in mind.) I myself think that the more helpful and illuminating way of conceiving and describing the situation is to regard Audi's view as belonging to a rather broad, but nonetheless distinct, family of views of which Locke's view is one member, Rawls's, another, and then Audi's a third. I propose revising my initial formulation, and henceforth thinking of *the liberal position* as incorporating the following as one of its core theses: citizens and officials are to base their decisions concerning (at least fundamental) political issues, and their discussion of those issues in the public space, on the principles yielded by some source independent of any and all of the religions to be found in society. This thesis Audi does accept, since it is silent on whether citizens and officials may *also* base their decisions and public discussions on *religious* considerations.

Audi's discussion is rich and contains much that is worth reflecting on. With a great deal of it I agree. But since I have to be selective, let me focus on the main point of disagreement between us—allowing a few other matters to come up along the way. That main point of disagreement is the thesis just mentioned: that it belongs to the ethic of the citizen in a liberal democracy to have an epistemologically adequate and motivationally sufficient basis for one's political discussions, decisions, and actions that is independent of each and every religion present in society. Audi embraces this understanding of the ethic of the citizen; I do not. I think the ethic of the citizen in a liberal democracy imposes no restrictions on the reasons people offer in their discussion of political issues in the public square, and likewise imposes none on the reasons they have for their political decisions and actions. If the position adopted, and the manner in which it is acted on, are compatible with the concept of liberal democracy, and if the discussion concerning the issue is conducted with civility, then citizens are free to offer and act on whatever reasons they find compelling. I regard it as an important implication of the concept of liberal democracy that citizens should have this freedom—that in this regard they should be allowed to act as they see fit. Liberal democracy implies, as I see it, that there should be no censorship in this regard.

In my discussion of the versions of the liberal position articulated by Locke and Rawls, I focused on two points: on the rationale offered for the independent-source thesis, and on the independent source proposed. Concerning the independent source, I posed three questions: is the source adequately identified, will it do the work

asked of it, and is it fair to ask all citizens and officials to appeal to
the principles yielded by this source as the basis for their discussions,
decisions, and actions on political matters? In my discussion of
Audi's version of the liberal position, I will focus almost entirely on
the rationale he offers, saying just a few things toward the end about
the source.

Audi's Version of the Liberal Position

It must be emphasized that when we have citizens in view,
rather than institutions, both Audi and I are discussing *the ethic of the
citizen* in a liberal democracy. Audi emphasizes that he is not discussing the *rights* of citizens; he is not, for example, claiming that the
religious person does not have a right to offer exclusively religious
reasons in public for his political positions, nor is he claiming that
the religious person does not have a right to base his political actions
entirely on such reasons. What he is claiming is that it is incompatible with the ethic of the citizen in a liberal democracy for the religious person to conduct himself or herself in that manner.

I fully agree with Audi in his insistence that our topic here is
not *rights*. However, when I emphasized that it was only *the ethic of
the citizen* that I was discussing, it was a somewhat different point
that I was concerned to make. Obviously it belongs to the ethic of
the citizen in a liberal democracy not to argue for and act on positions incompatible with the very concept of liberal democracy. But
as I observed, no actual society is fully a liberal democracy; each is
only *more or less* a liberal democracy. Furthermore, almost all citizens,
in any contemporary society that is for the most part a liberal democracy, believe that this is how it ought to be—though different
citizens have different views as to where their society should depart
from being a liberal democracy. For example, a great many Dutch,
English, and Danish people believe that their countries should continue to have a monarchy; but a monarchy, unless shorn of power
and privilege to the extent that it becomes nothing but a national
symbol, is incompatible with the concept of a liberal democracy.
Similarly, many English people believe that the Church of England
should continue to be established; but an established church is as

incompatible with the idea of a liberal democracy as anything could possibly be. Or consider the fact that in the United States there is wide support among the 'liberal' component of the citizenry for affirmative action. Affirmative action is quite clearly incompatible with the concept of a liberal democracy; it is, on the contrary, a strategy for undoing some of the consequences of our society's *not* having been a liberal democracy with respect to its treatment of women and people of color.

So once again: it is the ethic of the citizen in a liberal democracy that Audi and I are discussing. Whether a specific person, on a specific occasion, with respect to a specific issue, ought to practice that ethic, or whether she has a right not to practice it, is a different matter.

Incidentally, there is one point on which Audi and I appear to disagree in our conception of liberal democracy. Audi argues that the concept of liberal democracy incorporates what he calls *the libertarian principle*, the *equalitarian principle*, and the *neutral principle*. I agree. But as I observed in my initial contribution, what Audi calls "the equalitarian principle" is susceptible to two quite different interpretations, the *impartiality* interpretation and the *separation* interpretation, both interpretations being fully compatible with the concept of a liberal democracy. I went on to argue, however, that the separation interpretation, which says that the state shall do nothing to advance or hinder any or all religions, yields irresolvable dilemmas in our society and ought, on that ground, to be rejected in favor of the impartiality interpretation, which says that the state shall treat all religions and irreligions impartially. Audi, by contrast, takes the separation interpretation for granted—less obviously here, more obviously in some of his other articles. That is to say, he takes for granted, without considering the impartiality option, that it belongs to the very concept of a liberal democracy that the state will do nothing that is designed to advance or hinder any or all religions.

Before I engage the rationale that Audi offers for his version of the restraint on the use of religious reasons that the liberal position imposes, let me state what I take that version to be. Audi, to restate, is by no means urging the elimination of religious arguments for political positions. Not only does he think that religious arguments have a proper place in the lives of individuals and in the discourse of religious communities, he thinks they also have a legitimate place in the public space of civil society. In an earlier article, "The Place of Religious Argument in a Free and Democratic Society,"[1] he argues that there is nothing wrong about a person who has a religious argument for some political position *expressing* that point of view in the public space and *communicating* it to others. When the person is addressing his co-religionists, there is nothing wrong about going beyond expressing and communicating his point of view and using the argument to try to *persuade* his fellow believers of his position. In none of this, as Audi sees it—and of course I fully agree—is there anything incompatible with the ethic of the citizen in a liberal democracy.

Furthermore, the restraints that Audi proposes on the use of religious reasons are not meant for all laws and governmental policies whatsoever, but only for those which in some way constrict or coerce the conduct of citizens. It is true that most laws and governmental policies *do* constrict or coerce conduct—at least if we regard taxation as a form of constraint; thus, the scope of the restraint on the use of religious reasons that this qualification imposes is relatively minor. Nonetheless, the particular rationale that Audi offers for the restraint he proposes makes it important to have the qualification before us.

The restraint that Audi proposes on the use of religious reasons for political positions is this: A citizen must not advocate or support any coercive law or governmental policy, actual or prospective, unless that citizen has an adequate non-religious reason for that advocacy or support, unless that citizen is willing to offer that reason, and unless that citizen, beyond merely *having* that reason, is sufficiently *motivated* by it in his advocacy or support. The citizen may also *have* and *be motivated by* religious reasons; that is entirely acceptable. The citizen may present these reasons, not only to his fellow believers but in the public space; that too, as we saw above, is acceptable. But if the citizen does have religious reasons that motivate him, then he must *in addition* have non-religious reasons —"secular reasons," as Audi calls them—that have the epistemological status for the citizen of justifying his support or advocacy of the law or policy and the psychological status for the citizen of sufficiently motivating his support or advocacy.

Notice that the restriction Audi proposes makes no use of any public/private distinction; it differs in this respect from a good many other versions of the liberal position. Even if one never speaks up in the public space for the law or policy in question, *nevertheless,* if the law or policy is in any way coercive, one must have, and be sufficiently motivated by, adequate non-religious reasons for supporting or advocating it. To one's fellow believers, one may present religious reasons in addition; but then, one may do so in public as well. If one does present religious reasons in public, one must be able and willing to present, in addition, non-religious reasons that are justificationally adequate and motivationally sufficient, but one must be able and willing to offer such reasons to one's fellow believers as well.

Audi's Rationale

What arguments does Audi offer for the restraint he proposes? Several, including some that are explicitly formulated from the perspective of the religious person. The one on which I will focus most of my attention is the one to which Audi himself clearly assigns the most importance. It may be worth adding that in the background lies Audi's conviction that religious arguments are rather more dangerous than I think they are.

The essence of Audi's main argument—formulated early in that section of his initial contribution to this present discussion titled "Civic Virtue and Religious Conviction"—is that the very concept of a liberal democracy implies the restraint that he proposes. The *ethic of the citizen* in a liberal democracy incorporates this restriction because *the concept of a liberal democracy* implies this restriction.

Let us have Audi's own statement of the argument before us:

A liberal democracy by its very nature resists using coercion, and prefers persuasion, as a means to achieve cooperation. What we are persuaded, by being offered reasons, to do we tend to do autonomously and to identity with; what we are compelled to do we tend to resent doing. Thus, when there must be coercion, liberal democracies try to justify it in terms of considerations—such as public safety—that any fully rational adult citizen will find persuasive and can identify with. . . . If rational citizens in possession of the relevant facts cannot be persuaded of the necessity of the coercion—as is common where that coercion is based on an injunction grounded in someone else's religious scripture or revelation—then from the point of view of liberal democracy, it lacks an adequate basis. A liberal state exists in good part to accommodate a variety of people irrespective of their special preference for one kind of life over another; it thus allows coercion only where necessary to preserve civic order and not simply on the basis of majority preference. (30–31)

Before digging into the innards of this argument, let me call attention to some paradoxes that the position espoused engenders. In order to do so, let me distinguish between a *parliamentary session* and what I shall call a *quaker meeting*. A parliamentary session operates by majority vote—though it is essential to recognize that *majority* is not always to be equated with *simple plurality*. The assembly has rules for conducting discussions, making proposals, and so forth. Eventually, after appropriate discussion has occurred, a vote is taken; the will of the majority is regarded as the decision of the body. By contrast, a quaker meeting, as I shall understand it, operates by consensus; only if there is a consensus in favor of some proposal placed before the meeting is that proposal regarded as adopted by the body. By consensus here, I mean *agreement*, not *acquiescence*.[2] In the actual meetings of actual Quakers, a proposal is regarded as adopted by the body if no one says "no" to the proposal. What this means, in practice, is that the failure to say no to the proposal represents, on the part of some, acquiescence in the proposal rather than agreement with it. What I mean by a *quaker meeting* is a body that operates by *consensus*, that is, by *agreement*—not by agreement *plus* acquiescence.

Audi, along with a good many other defenders of one and another version of the liberal position, regards the concept of liberal democracy as incorporating the ideal of all the citizens together constituting a quaker meeting when it comes to the choosing of laws and governmental policies that are in any way coercive. In Audi's words, "A liberal democracy by its very nature resists using coercion, and prefers persuasion, as a means to achieve cooperation"

(16). Those proponents of liberal positions who share this view all acknowledge that the ideal cannot always be met; sometimes the disagreement among the citizenry is so firmly lodged that the citizens have to constitute themselves as a parliamentary session. But that, in the view of these proponents, represents a significant failure to measure up to the ideal embedded in the concept.

This failure to measure up to the ideal can, in principle, be conceptualized in either of two ways. One might say that insofar as the citizens constitute themselves as a parliamentary session rather than as a quaker meeting, just that far is that society not a liberal democracy. Alternatively, one might say that though this does not count against the society's being a liberal democracy, it makes of it a *malformed* liberal democracy—just as a tiger's loss of its tail in an accident does not transform it into a non-tiger but makes it a malformed tiger.

It appears to me that it is the former of these ways of conceptualizing the situation that Audi is working with. He says that "if fully rational citizens in possession of the relevant facts cannot be persuaded of the necessity of the coercion—as is common where that coercion is based on an injunction grounded in someone else's religious scripture or revelation—then from the point of view of liberal democracy, it lacks an adequate basis" (16). That sentence is compatible with both ways of conceptualizing the situation. The next one, however, tilts decisively toward the view that insofar as the citizens of some society constitute themselves as a parliamentary session rather than as a quaker meeting, just that far is that society not a liberal democracy at all; such behavior is incompatible with the very concept of a liberal democracy. This is what he says: "A liberal state exists in good part to accommodate a variety of people irrespective of their special preference for one kind of life over another; it thus allows coercion *only where necessary to preserve civic order and not simply on the basis of majority preference*" (16–17, italics added).

So much for my stylized distinction between a parliamentary assembly and a quaker meeting. I observed that Audi's position engenders a number of paradoxes. For one thing, no law or policy that I can think of, which has come up for discussion in the United States in recent years, has in fact enjoyed the consensus of all the (fully rational) citizenry; insofar as decisions have been taken on such matters, we the citizens have always functioned as a parliamentary session rather than as a quaker meeting. We have taken votes, and the will of the majority has been regarded as the decision of the body. The supposed ideal has not, in my memory, ever been attained; I see no reason to think that it ever will be attained.

That paradox generates another, derivative, paradox. Given that the quaker meeting is held out as the ideal *that we are to strive* for, citizens of liberal democracies, when dealing with coercive laws and policies, will, as Audi remarks, always try to justify their positions "in terms of considerations . . . that any fully rational adult citizen will find persuasive and can identify with" (16). If they fail in that endeavor, then, "from the point of view of liberal democracy," their advocacy "lacks an adequate basis." It seems to me that in our actual societies, anyone who embraced this position would simply refrain from advocating any position whatsoever on any issue of importance facing society. The pervasiveness of disagreement and controversy in our society constitutes overwhelming evidence for the conclusion that, on such issues, there simply are not any considerations that all adult citizens who are fully rational and adequately informed on the matter at hand will find persuasive and can identify with. The person who embraces Audi's view will, in her mind, run through a variety of considerations in support of some proposed law or policy; if she is at all socially observant, she will dismiss each one in succession, on the ground that almost certainly there is some citizen around who is fully rational and adequately informed on the matter but would not accept it. And so, she says nothing. That means, however, that she does not take part in the debate that leads up to the vote of the citizens constituted as a parliamentary session. And that is paradoxical: that embracing the position Audi favors would lead one to be silent in our parliamentary sessions.

Paradoxes, I have called these. The understanding of liberal democracy with which Audi is working implies that, in a well-formed liberal democracy, all decisions will be made by the full consensus of the citizens who are fully rational and adequately informed on the matter. The fact that that understanding generates these paradoxes indicates to me that a different understanding of liberal democracy is required. For as a matter of fact, a pervasive and prominent feature of any society that anyone would ever pick out as very much a liberal democracy is the taking of decisions by majority vote. How, then, can it be right to say that this is a point of malformation in the liberal democratic character of those societies—or alternatively, that such societies are in this respect not liberal democracies at all? If one's understanding of the concept of liberal democracy yields the conclusion that majority votes are incompatible with a society's being a well-formed liberal democracy, should one not then rethink one's understanding of the concept?

But whereas I interpret these paradoxes as indicators that something has gone wrong in Audi's understanding of the concept of liberal democracy, he, if he sticks to his guns, will interpret them as mere paradoxes, nothing more. Let me, then, go beyond pointing to these paradoxical implications of Audi's position to consider the argument he offers. Why does Audi think that the concept of liberal democracy really does incorporate this ideal?

I wish he were more explicit on this point than he is, since this is really the central issue between us. But I think I see how he is thinking. A liberal democratic state, he says, "exists in good part to accommodate a variety of people irrespective of their special preference for one kind of life over another" (16). Within the constraints of the necessity "to preserve civic order," it is committed to allowing all citizens to live their lives autonomously—to allowing all citizens to pursue their particular vision of the good life as they see fit. But if some coercive law or policy is proposed that certain citizens oppose, and if that law is instituted by majority vote in parliamentary session of the citizenry, then the autonomy of those who are in opposition is restricted. They are not allowed to live as they see fit. And that is incompatible with the fundamental commitment underlying the liberal democratic form of state. Such restriction may be necessary "to preserve civic order." But it must be seen for what it is: infringing on the autonomy of those who oppose the law or policy. So if I advocate or support a law or policy that I know, or have good reason to believe, some citizens oppose, then I am advocating or supporting an infringement on their autonomy; thereby I am acting in violation of the very concept of a liberal democracy. I take it that this, plus a few small qualifications, is Audi's argument.

In that other article of his to which I have already called attention, "The Place of Religious Argument in a Free and Democratic

Society," Audi develops a slightly different take on the argument. There he suggests that embedded in the concept of liberal democracy is a certain understanding of the conditions under which coercion is legitimate. That understanding can be formulated thus: "we can coerce people to do only what they would autonomously do if appropriately informed and fully rational" (689). He goes on to remark that this understanding of justified coercion "explains why justified coercion is not *resented* by agents when they adequately understand its rationale, why some coercion is consonant with liberal democratic ideals of autonomy, and why the kind that is can be supported by citizens *independently* of what they happen to approve of politically, religiously, or, to a large extent, even morally" (689–90).

Both in his "Place of Religious Argument" article and in his initial contribution to this present discussion, Audi develops his argument almost entirely from the standpoint of one who is analyzing the concept of liberal democracy. In the conclusion of the former of these articles he steps briefly out of that standpoint into the standpoint of the moralist. What he then says supplements nicely what we have heard him saying thus far:

> I think that sound ethics itself dictates that, out of respect for others as free and dignified individuals, we should always have and be sufficiently motivated by adequate secular reasons for our positions on those matters of law or public policy in which our decisions might significantly restrict human freedom. If you are fully rational and I cannot convince you of my view by arguments framed in the concepts we share as rational beings, then even if mine is the majority view I should not coerce you. Perhaps the political system under which we live embodies a legal right for the majority to do so, for certain ranges of conduct; perhaps there is even a moral right to do so, given our mutual understanding of majority rule. But the principles I am suggesting still make a plausible claim on our allegiance. (701)

What is new here is the suggestion that the principles of adequate secular rationale and of sufficient secular motivation are not only implications of the concept of liberal democracy, but are required by the respect that we ought to show others as "free and dignified individuals." Liberal democracy is not a freestanding, happenstance, development; it has an ethical basis.

Evaluation of the Rationale

So what about Audi's rationale for the restraint he proposes on the use of religious reasons? Note, in the first place, that the rationale he offers implies a similar restriction on a vast array of other reasons as well. Indeed, the rationale speaks not so much to *arguments* and *reasons* for political positions as to those positions themselves. The concept of a well-formed liberal democratic society, Audi says, is that of a society so structured that the citizens will be free to act autonomously except insofar as the need for civic order requires restriction on such freedom. And if, for some coercive law or policy of some more or less liberal democratic state, there are fully rational and appropriately informed citizens who disagree with that law or policy, then their autonomy is infringed upon. Accordingly, the ethic of the citizen in a liberal democracy requires that one only support and advocate laws and policies that enjoy, or would enjoy, the consensus of all appropriately informed and fully rational citizens. Obviously, this has implications for the espousing of 'sectarian' religious positions and for the offering of religious reasons. Audi focuses on those. But the ramifications are vastly wider. The classification with which Audi works, *religious reasons* versus *secular reasons*, though appropriate for his purposes, is nonetheless misleading. The classification that the rationale calls for is that between reasons that would be accepted by all appropriately informed and fully rational citizens, and those that would not be accepted by all such. And as already observed, it is not even *reasons* that are of immediate concern but *conclusions—positions*.

The core of the argument is straightforward: If someone is coerced by a law or policy that he disagrees with, then his autonomy is thereby infringed upon, whereas the concept of a liberal democracy is the concept of a social/political arrangement that is committed to giving all citizens the freedom to live autonomously—within the boundaries of whatever might be required for civic order. I see no reason to question the first premise; it is the second one that I contest. The disagreement between Audi and myself pivots on our divergent understandings of the concept of liberal democracy. Unfortunately, it is not easy to find solid rock here; everything seems to be shifting sand. But let me do my best.

Audi's understanding of the concept of liberal democracy, to repeat, is that it is that form of social arrangement in which everyone is free to live autonomously except insofar as the necessities of civic order require otherwise. It is that form of social arrangement in which no one is coerced except by such laws and policies as he or she would agree to were he or she appropriately informed and fully rational on the matter. My reason for thinking that this understanding is not correct is that, if it were correct, the concept would be *nowhere near* being exemplified *anywhere*. No society would be anywhere near being a liberal democracy. Yet the concept originated—or so at least I assume—not from the speculations of theorists concerning ideal types of social order, but from the attempts of theorists to single out certain extant societies from others as constituting a certain type, the liberal democratic type. Or more precisely: to identify a certain continuum exhibited by extant societies, viz., the continuum ranging from societies that are scarcely at all liberal democratic in character to those that are very much liberal democratic in character.

One of the hallmarks which has regularly been used for placing societies on that continuum is that of equal voice for all citizens within fair voting procedures, with the will of the majority being regarded as the decision of the body. A correlative hallmark of the liberal democratic society is its constitutional, or quasi-constitutional, guarantee of the rights of minorities: certain social arrangements are insulated against the will of the majority.

Contrast Audi's understanding of the concept of liberal democracy—and Audi on this matter is typical of current exponents of the liberal position. On his understanding, the use of voting procedures in which the will of the majority is the determinant of the body's decision *counts against* that society's being liberal democratic in character. Insofar as decisions are taken in the manner of the parliamentary session rather than in the manner of the quaker meeting, just insofar is that society *not* liberal democratic in character.

Someone might reply with the following question: be all that as it may, isn't Audi nonetheless right in his suggestion that the concept of a liberal democracy has *something to do with* citizens being allowed to live their lives as they see fit—*something to do with* citizens being allowed, in that sense, to live their lives autonomously?

I think he is right in that suggestion. Thus, it turns out that everything pivots on the right understanding of "something to do with." My own attempt to formulate the concept of a liberal democracy went as follows: Equal protection under law for all people, equal freedom in law for all citizens, neutrality on the part of the state with respect to the diversity of religious and other comprehensive perspectives present in society, and equal voice for all citizens within fair voting schemes. The second clause indicates that I, too, regard liberal democracy as having *something to do with* autonomy; *something to do with* the freedom of citizens to live their lives as they see fit. Exactly what that freedom comes to, however, seems to me exceedingly difficult to formulate—or even to understand. I have myself not yet succeeded in understanding and formulating it. In my original contribution I contented myself with speaking of *equal freedom*—all the while silently acknowledging that to speak thus is to do no more than point in the direction where, so I surmise, adequate understanding and formulation lies.

In short, though I agree that some sort of autonomy principle is embedded in the concept of liberal democracy, I do not, for the reasons given, think that it is the one that Audi proposes. And since the main rationale he gives, for the restraint on the use of religious reasons that he proposes, depends crucially on his understanding of the concept of liberal democracy and the autonomy principle embedded therein, I conclude that the defense he mounts, of that version of the liberal position which he embraces, is no better than the defenses offered of the versions embraced by Locke and Rawls.

What, then, about the ethical argument that Audi offers, to the effect that respect for others as free and dignified individuals requires that we not support coercing them except for reasons they would accept if they were fully rational and adequately informed? Here I have little to say beyond what I said in my initial contribution. When it comes to what is required for showing respect, I think we must consider the situation not only from the speaker's perspective but also from the hearer's. To show full respect for you, as a free and dignified individual, requires, without imposing any restrictions on the content of your speech, inviting you to tell me how you see the situation and then to listen. To listen with the goal in mind of learning from you. To listen also with the goal in mind of discerning how I can communicate to you my own perspective and perhaps persuade you of its cogency. But beyond that, to listen for what I can learn from you. Thus, to make up my own mind in the light of what you say—*whatever it is* that you say. That, it seems to me, is what is required by showing respect in such matters.

Is the situation different if coercion is in the background? I fail to see that it is. Suppose that some law or policy with coercive import is under consideration. We each state our view on the matter—saying whatever we want to say. We each listen to the other and make our final decision in the light of what we have heard. Then we vote. If I lose in the vote, then, though I do not agree, I *acquiesce*—unless I find the decision truly appalling. I do not like the decision; I prefer that it have gone the other way. But I have been allowed to say whatever I wanted to say, and I have been heard, genuinely heard. Is there anything more that I can ask of you by way of respect?

That I am coerced by a law that I oppose—is that not, per se, an indication that I am not being accorded full respect as a free and dignified individual? In a way, yes. But here we have to be reminded of the Augustinian point: we are talking about the politics of earthly cities, not about the politics of the heavenly city.

Let me conclude these reflections on the rationale that Audi offers for the restriction he proposes on the use of religious reasons with two small additional points. Audi holds that, when it comes to advocating or supporting coercive laws or policies, we should be sure to have reasons that all our fellow citizens would accept if adequately informed and fully rational. This, he holds, is a central component in the ethic of the citizen in a liberal democracy. But why the qualification, *fully rational?* Suppose that some citizen who holds an opposing view to mine on some prospective law or policy did not arrive at his position in a fully rational manner. What difference does that make? If respect for a person as free and dignified requires, when the person is fully rational on the issue, that I not advocate a coercive policy to which he is opposed, why is it different when the person is not fully rational on the matter? After all, the right of individuals to 'voice' in liberal democracies is not conditioned on whether they have arrived at their positions in a fully rational manner. Rationality is not among the requirements one must satisfy to be entitled to vote. Similarly, whatever the exact nature of the commitment to autonomy that is embedded in the concept of liberal democracy, surely that commitment is not limited in its application to those citizens who arrive at their positions rationally. The insertion of epistemological stipulations at this point seems to me out of accord with the nature of liberal democracy.

Second, what is this concept of the *fully rational* to which Audi appeals? Audi appears to be of the view that if we all only reflect on issues in a fully rational manner, then, if we are also adequately informed, we will arrive at a consensus substantial enough to serve as the basis for political decisions in a complex liberal democratic society. The assumption seems to be that rationality will both winnow out diversity and leave sufficient consensus to serve as the basis of decisions on political matters. Thus, in spite of his sophistication on epistemological matters, Audi appears to me to be resuscitating something very much like the Lockean perspective—which, so I argued in my initial contribution, is unacceptable. So, I say, it appears to me; it may very well be that I am misinterpreting him on this point.

Audi's Independent Source

My comments on the independent source that Audi proposes will be relatively brief. Fundamentally, the source is simply the stock of principles that any adequately informed and fully rational adult member of one's society would accept; one's support and advocacy of coercive policies and legislation must be adequately justified and sufficiently motivated by one's acceptance of those. In our pluralistic societies, this implies that the principles will have to be what Audi calls "secular"; our advocacy and support will have to be based on 'secular reasons.'

What is a secular reason? In his "Place of Religious Argument" article, Audi formulates the concept thus: "A secular reason is roughly one whose normative force does not evidentially depend on the existence [or non-existence] of God or on theological considerations, or on the pronouncements of a person or institution qua religious authority" (692). I understand this to amount to the following: a reason is secular for a given person if the evidence on the basis of which that person believes that reason entails neither the existence nor non-existence of God, neither the acceptance nor rejection of some person or institution as religious authority, nor any theological proposition.

I find the application of this concept considerably more difficult and problematic than Audi appears to find it. Let me speak personally at this point—as a religious believer. In the United States, welfare is regularly thought of in terms of charity; the question typically under debate is the extent to which the government should engage in those charitable acts that constitute welfare. By contrast, I think the basic issue involved in welfare is an issue of *rights*; I think everybody has a *right* to fair access to means of sustenance. I have come to believe this by reflecting on what the biblical writers say about the poor.

Do I also have a secular reason for believing that there is this right? I am not sure. Suppose I get into a dispute with someone on some detail of welfare policy, and I announce to him that the principle on which I am basing my position is that everybody has a right to fair access to means of sustenance. Is that principle a secular reason? After all, it entails nothing at all about the existence or non-existence of God, about religious authorities, or anything of the sort. And let us suppose that it does adequately justify and sufficiently motivate my advocacy of the position in question—as it well may.

If I at all understand Audi's thought here, his answer is no, this is not a secular reason—not for me, anyway. If this counted as a secular reason, religious people would almost always automatically have secular reasons. The religious person opposed to abortion *because God says that abortion is wrong* is perforce also opposed to abortion *because abortion is wrong*. To determine whether someone's reason is secular or not, one cannot simply look at the reason in isolation; one has to look at its "evidential dependence." And that, of course, varies to a considerable degree from person to person. Audi speaks of various "paths" to the same moral truths. To determine whether or not someone's reason is secular, one usually has to know the path by which it was arrived at; usually it will not be sufficient to scrutinize it for its entailments. (Though there is, as I see it, considerable tension in Audi's thought at this point. The rationale that Audi gives for the restraint on the reasons that he proposes speaks not at all about the path whereby I arrived at the moral principle in question, but only about whether my fellow citizens would accept the principle if fully rational and adequately informed.)

So once again, do I have a secular reason for my conviction that people have a *right* to fair access to means of sustenance? I am not at all sure; I find it difficult to tell—mainly because I find the application in this context of the concept of evidence deeply problematic. Do most people have *evidence* for their fundamental moral convictions? I doubt it. So far as I can tell, however, I do not have a secular reason for that rights principle. I came to believe it by reflecting on the message of the Old Testament prophets and the New Testament Gospels; if I have evidence for it, that is the evidence.

Could I *devise* a secular reason for it? Might some moral philosophy, such as Kantianism, utilitarianism, or intuitionism provide the resources for an argument? Utilitarianism seems to me highly unpromising, and intuitionism is beside the point, since it says that our access to fundamental moral principles is by intuition, not by argumentation. Of all the secular options, Kantianism looks the most promising. I rather think I could devise a Kantian argument for my conviction about the right to fair access to means of sustenance—though I am not sure, since I have never tried. I am absolutely sure, however, that most of my fellow believers could not devise such an argument, since most of them either do not know about Kantianism, or if they do, do not understand it. So if that is what is required, in this regard, by the ethic of the citizen in a liberal democracy, for most people it is a very onerous requirement indeed.

In short, my difficulty with Audi's notion of secular reasons is this: either the religious person almost automatically has secular reasons along with religious reasons for his political positions, or it is going to be very difficult for him to acquire those reasons.

Audi argues that an omnipotent and omnibenevolent God would surely provide secular paths to important moral truths as well as religious paths—evidential paths, that is, not only pedagogical paths. Maybe so. But can we also infer that the secular paths will be of such a sort that almost all citizens will be able to find them and travel on them? And in any case—now to use explicitly theological language—to argue thus is to think exclusively in terms of creation, not at all in terms of fallenness. We do not exist in a pristine state. We all live east of Eden. We, one and all, are all mucked up, not only in our actions but in our beliefs on moral matters. Though God may indeed have provided paths, we have all, like sheep, gone astray.

In Summary

I see no reason, then, to depart from my original position. The ethic of the citizen in a liberal democracy does impose definite restrictions on the laws and policies that citizens support and advocate; certain laws and policies would be inconsistent with the very concept of a liberal democracy. Likewise, the ethic of the citizen imposes definite restrictions on the manner in which citizens conduct their discussions and debates. But the ethic of the citizen imposes no restraints on the reasons citizens offer for their positions—except such restraints as may be implied by the restrictions on position and manner. To the contrary: it implies that there are no such restraints. At this point, citizens are free to live their lives as they see fit.

Let religious people use what reasons they wish, and offer them to whomever they wish. Let non-religious people do so as well. Of course, if the religious person wants to *persuade* the non-religious person, or the person of another religion, of his position, he will have to do more than offer his own idiosyncratic religious reasons. But that is a requirement of strategy, not a requirement embodied in the ethic of the citizen in a liberal democracy.

A final comment. It is customary, in academic writing, to conceal oneself behind the abstractions of the discourse. But Robert Audi and I are personal friends who, while agreeing on very many matters, have our disagreements on this one. So let me say, in closing, that I hope and trust that we have so conducted ourselves here that our discussion is a model of how friends can vigorously debate their points of disagreement in public and remain friends! To which I may add that, whatever our disagreements about the details of liberal democracy, this much we definitely agree on: it is essential to liberal democracy that it accord citizens the freedom to debate in public which restraints, if any, the ethic of the citizen in a liberal democracy places on the use, by citizens, of religious reasons.

Notes

1. *San Diego Law Review* 30, no. 4 (Fall 1993): pp. 685–6.
2. There is a very insightful discussion concerning the importance of distinguishing between agreement and *acquiescence* in Nicholas Rescher, *Pluralism: Against the Demand for Consensus* (Oxford: Clarendon Press, 1993).

RELIGION, POLITICS, AND DEMOCRACY: CLOSING COMMENTS AND REMAINING ISSUES

Robert Audi

It is appropriate for a volume of this kind to have a closing statement that highlights some major issues and some of the main points of agreement and disagreement between the authors. Professor Wolterstorff suggested that I write such a statement, in part out of a conscientious concern about his interpretation of my essay and of one I published in 1993. (Producing a coauthored statement was not possible within our tight schedule.) What follows is mainly intended to advance discussion of the overall problem that concerns us both: the place of religious convictions in the political realm in a liberal democracy. But I will also bring out similarities and differences between our positions and, in the light of some of his remarks, clarify my own view.

The Scope of Impartiality

Wolterstorff does well to recur to the question of what, in a liberal democracy, constitutes an appropriate governmental impartiality regarding religion. He sees impartiality *among* religions as crucial for liberal democratic governments; I favor impartiality *regarding* religion, and I contend that it implies neutrality toward religion. I grant, however, that the freedom to practice one's religion is central for liberal democracy. I hold, then, that governmental *indifference* toward religion is inappropriate to a liberal democracy. I believe this is a point of strong agreement between us.

A basic question that remains is how a government can be attentive to the preservation of religious liberty and in other ways concerned with religion, yet neutral toward it in the sense that requires giving no preference to the religious as such over the nonreligious. I think this is possible and indeed that neutrality allows governmental actions with the *effect*, as opposed to the purpose, of promoting religious practice. But a great deal remains to be said about just what impartiality and neutrality mean in this context and about how, in practice, a government should realize these two ideals.

Consensus versus Majority Preference as Democratic Standards

I welcome Wolterstorff's introducing this distinction and the related contrast between consensus and mere agreement. He is correct, moreover, in suggesting that I believe consensus in sociopolitical decisions is better, other things equal, than mere agreement, especially where agreement is achieved only by a bare majority vote. I have not implied, however, that only consensus can justify such decisions. This is particularly so if consensus entails *unanimity*. I do not think Wolterstorff holds that it requires unanimity, but it is important to see that it does not. Perfect consensus does; but particularly in large groups, consensus can be reached where there are abstentions or even a limited number of dissenters of certain sorts.

The wider issue here is what kind of basis democratic decisions should have, particularly if they involve coercion of citizens. Wolterstorff and I agree that not just any basis is ethically acceptable; selfish desires, for instance, are not. The main difference between us here is in the indispensable role I give to secular reasons by contrast with his permissiveness toward religious reasons as capable of properly underlying one's entire sociopolitical stance. My position (to date) is that this indispensability thesis is plausible *both* on general grounds of political philosophy and from the point of view of protecting religious liberty, a point of view that is appropriate for churches as well as governments and the general public. I believe

Wolterstorff has greater doubts about the former claim than the latter; but he has some doubt about that too.

Although the fourth section of his critique suggests that believers can commonly find some secular reason for sociopolitical action, my requirement of adequate reasons is unclear to him. I have meant to invoke only a broad notion of adequacy not requiring conceptual sophistication as a condition of having an adequate reason. But this is a large issue deserving far more discussion than we can give it in this book (I return to the issue below, and there are references in my initial essay to my own and others' work on justification and reasons).

The Justification of Coercion

This is a very large and highly complex problem. Wolterstorff is quite right to push my view to its apparent limits. He does this, however, not by taking off from the principles of secular rationale or motivation but from a wider statement I made (beginning in the 1993 paper) about the basis of liberal democracy. This is perfectly fair, but I would stress that those principles are intended to be compatible with various differing accounts of the basis of liberal democracy, and they may be sound even if I went too far in suggesting that a liberal society allows coercion only where necessary to preserve civic order. (This certainly would go too far if the reference were to what is in fact allowed and not to what comports with the ideals of a liberal society.)

The pressing question Wolterstorff raises here is (in my mind) this: May we take the notion of civic order broadly enough to make the suggested constraint on the use of coercion in a liberal democracy reasonable in the ideal case? It will help to recall the distinction (made on p. 25 of my essay) between primary and secondary coercion and to apply the constraint wholly or mainly to the former, say to having a system of taxation at all as opposed to spending tax dollars on health care rather than space exploration. But Wolterstorff would still reject the constraint, in part on the ground that the condition for meeting it—that (fully) rational citizens in possession of the relevant facts can be persuaded of the law or policy in question—is too strict. He contends that for essentially any proposed law or policy an observant citizen "will dismiss each one . . . on the ground that almost certainly there is some (rational) citizen around who would not accept it" (154). This is plausible but neglects the requirement that the dissenter be adequately *informed* (possess "the relevant facts"). No doubt Wolterstorff would note that the concept of relevant facts is problematic, and he might argue that one would expect significant dissent even if those concerned are both fully rational and adequately informed. This remains a deep issue. Let me bring out some of its elements needing future exploration.

Ethical theorists have disputed whether people who are rational (hence not confused, logically deficient, etc.) and agree on all the relevant facts can disagree morally. Those who think not may be proceeding on the idea (noted in my essay where supervenience is described, p. 19) that moral properties are determined by non-moral ones—roughly by "facts." But what about, say, abortion? It *seems* that people can agree on all the biological and other pertinent facts and still differ over whether the zygote at conception is a person (where that notion is assumed to be in part moral). Must some of them be lacking in rationality?

This is an issue well worth pondering—though my commitment in this book is at most to the narrower view that fully rational, adequately informed people will agree on the justifiability of certain bases of governmental *coercion* (such as public safety). I do not propose a resolution of the issue of whether moral disagreement is possible for fully rational persons who agree on all the relevant facts, but my position concerning the kind of coercion in question is that citizens have a prima facie obligation not to advocate or support it without having evidentially adequate and motivationally sufficient secular reason for it. One would think that on being offered an evidentially *adequate* reason, fully rational persons in possession of the relevant facts would agree to the conclusion in question— though there are further conditions, such as the clarity with which the reason is presented and the reflectiveness of the audience; and with many issues, including abortion, there are difficulties about how to determine what range of facts is relevant. Moreover, if one believes that there are fully rational, adequately informed people who think that the zygote or early fetus is not a person, then as a conscientious citizen in a liberal democracy, prohibiting them from seeking (certain) abortions is something one should be at least reluctant to do, and it would appear that the government in a liberal democracy will resist doing it. I leave open that there could be some theological fact that entails that there is a particular point where personhood occurs in the human life cycle; but my point here—not dependent on the idea that coercion requires agreement of the (fully) rational and adequately informed—is that a liberal democracy will not coerce on a theological basis either, in part in the interest of preserving, in addition to civic order, *religious* liberty.

Suppose, however, that justified coercion does require the hypothetical agreement just described. Must we then say, as Wolterstorff suggests we must, that the use of majority vote to determine decisions "*counts against* that society's being liberal democratic in character" (158). Much depends on what constraints there are: if absolutely anything can be done should the majority want it, the society is not a liberal democracy, since basic rights to (e.g.) freedom would be cancelable; if the majority abides by a suitable constitution or certain standards, the society may be a liberal democracy. Granted, a liberal democracy may fail to meet its standards and so may, for instance, coerce school children into prayer sessions despite the presence of rational, adequately informed people who reject the practice. My suggestion is that such a society is committed to resisting this kind of coercion and—more important—that virtuous citizens are prima facie obligated not to support it without an adequate secular reason.

This is a good place to note a difference between Wolterstorff and me concerning the essentials of liberal democracy. He stresses equal protection under the law, equal freedom for all citizens, state neutrality among religions and other comprehensive views, and equal voting rights (159). I agree with him here but stress the need for an optimum *level* of freedom. *Equal* freedom is possible even when there is too little of it. We agree that restrictions need special justifications; but I defend stronger criteria than he does for justifying such restrictions. One is reminded of the common contrast between the French democratic tradition, largely centering on equality, and the English democratic tradition, largely centering on liberty. We agree that equality, of the right sort, *and* liberty, at the right level, are essential in liberal democracy. We differ in how we conceive them and their interrelations.

Liberal Democracy and Mutual Respect

Given the importance of respect for persons as a central notion in ethics, it is no surprise that it surfaces in this book as an important element in citizenship. I have stressed the sense in which liberal democratic citizenship—and liberal democratic government— should embody such respect in constraining the coercion of others; Wolterstorff emphasizes something that I would call *empathic civility*. We are to listen to others to try to understand, to communicate our perspective, and to learn from them and take account of their views in making our own decisions (160). I welcome his emphasis on these sound points. But we differ on whether the situation changes and (in my view) demands a higher standard of toleration when coercion is at stake, particularly primary coercion, as with conscription, compulsory education, and inoculations. "If I lose in the vote," he says, "then, though I do not agree, I *acquiesce*—unless I find the decision truly appalling" (160). My position is designed in part to reduce the chance that those who are outvoted will merely acquiesce or, especially, that those who are coerced in some important matter will find the majority decision truly appalling. I think it is not likely that this will happen when both they and those enforcing a law or policy are fully rational and adequately informed.

It may seem that my position implies that rationality is a requirement one must satisfy to have a right to vote in a liberal democracy (as Wolterstorff might be read as suggesting on 160). But it does not, and we are agreed that the crucial topic of our exchange is the ethics of citizenship construed as encompassing more than the subject of the rights of citizens (though that is part of it). I take citizens in a liberal democracy to have a prima facie obligation to have adequate secular reason for advocacy or support of coercive laws or public policies; but that minimal rationality condition is necessary only for exercising civic virtue, not for a right to vote.

Secular Reasons and Secular Motivation

A major question raised by any approach to constraining reliance on religious considerations in democracy is what they are and how the constraints on them work. Wolterstorff's essay and critique are instructive on this, but his critique makes my view sound considerably further from his than it is. He says that a religious person opposed to abortion because God says it is wrong is "perforce" opposed to it because it is wrong (162).

I agree that if God says it is wrong, then it is wrong and that this is a secular moral judgment. But *believing* God says it is wrong does not entail being secularly *motivated* by this secular judgment. Because God says it is wrong, one might *both* believe it is wrong and oppose it; this is different from being opposed to it *because* it is wrong (thus on a moral ground), and it is consistent with having no reason or motive for the opposition independently of one's theology. The not unnatural interpretation Wolterstorff gives here runs together considerations of rationale with considerations of motivation. If he were observing that distinction (whose importance is one reason I propose different principles for rationale and motivation), he should have no doubt that, in virtue of holding the relevant moral judgment, one would have a secular reason to oppose abortion. We agree, in any event, that there can be religious reasons for secular moral judgments and that the latter can motivate independently. We differ in that I hold that they *should* motivate independently in certain kinds of coercion (e.g. instituting mandatory prayer sessions in public schools), and he denies this.

We also agree that people can find secular reasons for various sociopolitical views even if they arrive at them from religious grounds. But he underestimates the extent of our agreement—or at least the breadth of the category of secular reason—when he rules out intuitionism as "beside the point, since it says that our access to fundamental moral principles is by intuition, not argumentation" (163). For me, judging that an action is morally wrong counts as having a reason to oppose it; one need not have a further reason—roughly a premise—for this judgment, religious or secular. To require that would beg the question against even a minimal foundationalism, which would insist that there can be rational judgments that need no premises and are rational on the basis of, say, perceptual experience or rational insight. To be sure, a reason not supported by a premise might not be adequate. But I believe this is not how morality works in all cases, nor is liberalism committed to taking it to work so: that enslaving someone is wrong, or that beating people for sadistic pleasure is outrageous, may be adequate reasons not to do such things, whether there is any deeper reason or not.

One of the profound questions that this latitude about moral reasons raises is why, if reasons can rest on grounds other than premises, religious reasons need be constrained in a liberal democracy. My answer is *not* that there cannot be evidentially cogent religious grounds (a further point of agreement with Wolterstorff), but that the ethics appropriate to a liberal democracy constrains religious considerations (and doubtless other kinds) because of its commitment to preserving the liberty of all. It imposes a prima facie obligation not to restrict the conduct of citizens unless there are reasons for the restriction that are appropriate to any of the fully rational, adequately informed citizens irrespective of their religious commitments.

The vitality of a free and democratic society depends on its ability to achieve cooperation among diverse peoples, to inspire among its citizens loyalty to its ideals and to each other, and to accommodate religious and other practices central in the lives of its people. Citizens with far-reaching religious commitments will have a vision of human life as it ought to be, and they quite properly seek to shape their society accordingly. Democratic governments must reconcile differences, preserve order, and provide services to the people. This requires a kind of impartiality among citizens and institutions. But democratic governments are of, by, and for the people. If we the people are quite properly directed by our own ideals, how can we reasonably be asked, as electors of our government or holders of its offices, to exercise restraint regarding those very ideals, and how is such restraint to be understood and realized? The question becomes even more urgent when the ideals are religious and are seen as representing divine wisdom. This is the chief question that has occupied Wolterstorff and me here. It will continue to occupy us and many others long into the future.

INDEX

abortion, ix, 2, 29, 30, 31, 34, 41, 49, 51, 59n25, 60n35, 64n56, 104, 126, 127, 162, 170–71, 173
Ackerman, Bruce, 59n26
affirmative action, 127, 149
agapism, 22, 59n27
aid to the poor, 11, 12, 14, 22, 56n10, 124, 127
Alston, William 55n5
Aquinas, Thomas, 10, 24
Archbishop of Canterbury, 7
Aristotle, 33, 37, 59n28

biblical criticism, 90

Carter, Stephen, 59n26, 62n42, 64n55
Christian Environment Council, 112, 140–41
Christianity, 5, 17, 124. *See also* Hebraic-Christian tradition; religion
church-state issues: impartiality of the state, x, 4, 5–6, 70, 76, 115, 122, 149, 167; neutrality of the church, 39–47, 49, 64n53; neutrality of the state, ix, 4, 6–8, 38, 55n6, 70–71, 75–77, 115, 122, 127–28, 144n4, 149, 159, 167; separation of, ix–x, 2–8, 38–47, 54, 76, 142–43. *See also* liberal democracy; liberalism; religious liberty
citizenship, x, 63n51; epistemological restraint and, 15, 69, 73, 77; ethics of, 17, 54, 67–69, 76–77, 93–95, 109–13, 117, 130, 133–38, 142–43, 147–49, 151, 157, 159–60, 164–65, 174. *See also* civic virtue; civility; liberal democracy; theo-ethical equilibrium

civic virtue, 10, 16, 21, 24, 54; public discourse and, 33–35, 49–50, 53, 55, 62n45, 62n46, 75, 79, 96, 101, 106–8, 110–14, 132–33, 135–38, 144n9, 149–51, 159–60; religious reasoning and, ix, x, 16, 30–31, 35, 39–42, 46, 49, 52–53, 57, 64n55, 73, 77, 86, 112, 123, 129–30, 138, 140–41, 149–50, 157; religious virtue and, 16, 23, 36; secular motivation and, 28–33, 37, 48–53, 61n36, 61n39, 122, 137–38, 173; secular reasoning and, 13–15, 17, 25–28, 30, 33, 36–37, 48–53, 73, 75, 122–23, 126, 137–38, 140–41, 150, 157, 161–62, 173. *See also* citizenship; civility; respect; virtue ethics
civility, 112–13, 139, 143, 147, 172
coercion, 21, 30, 32, 33, 51, 94, 96, 133, 150–56, 168–70; acquiescence and, 152, 172; persuasion and, 16, 108, 152; primary and secondary, 25–26. *See also* taxation; voting
communism, 7, 80; churches and, 45, 119n1
consociality, 81, 114–15

Darwinism, 90
Declaration of Independence, 65n66
Dewey, John, 62n43, 144n5
disarmament, 44
divine commands, 10–11, 22–23, 31, 57n20, 58n21, 58n23, 141

Elshtain, Jean Bethke, 63n51
epistemology, 82–90, 121, 173–74; fallibilism, 15, 57n15, 82, 88; "Reformed," 87, 129–30, 144n6. *See also*

ABOUT THE AUTHORS

Robert Audi writes and teaches in the areas of ethics, political philosophy, the theory of knowledge, the philosophy of mind, and the philosophy of religion. His books include *Rationality, Religious Belief, and Moral Commitment* (1986), *Practical Reasoning* (1989), *Action, Intention, and Reason* (1993), *The Structure of Justification* (1993), and *The Cambridge Dictionary of Philosophy* (1995), for which he was Editor-in-Chief. His *Moral Knowledge and Ethical Character* will appear in 1997, and *The Problems of Epistemology* is scheduled to appear in 1998. He has served as Editor-in-Chief of the *Journal of Philosophical Research,* and under grants from the National Endowment for the Humanities he has directed institutes and seminars for faculty from colleges and universities nationwide. He received his B.A. from Colgate University in 1963 with majors in philosophy and English and his Ph.D. in 1967 from the University of Michigan. He has been president of the American Philosophical Association (Central Division) and is currently the Charles J. Mach Distinguished Professor of Philosophy at the University of Nebraska, Lincoln.

Nicholas Wolterstorff received his B.A. degree from Calvin College and his M.A. and Ph.D. from Harvard University, in philosophy. After teaching for two years at Yale University, he returned to his alma mater, Calvin College, where he taught philosophy for 30 years. Currently he is at Yale, as Noah Porter Professor of Philosophical Theology in the Divinity School, and as adjunct professor in the Philosophy Department and the Religious Studies Department. He has taught, for one- or two-semester stints, at Haverford College, Notre Dame University, Princeton University, the University of Texas, the University of Michigan, Temple University, and the Free University of Amsterdam. He has been president of the American Philosophical Association (Central Division) and of the Society of Christian Philosophers.

After beginning his career concentrating on metaphysics (*On Universals*), he spent some time working on aesthetics (*Works and*

Worlds of Art, Art in Action). In more recent years, he has been working in epistemology (*John Locke and the Ethics of Belief*), philosophy of religion (*Divine Discourse*), and political philosophy (*Until Justice and Peace Embrace*).

In the fall of 1993 he gave the Wilde Lectures at Oxford University: these constitute the core of *Divine Discourse*. In the spring of 1995 he gave the Gifford Lectures at St. Andrews University. These lectures, on epistemology, will appear under the title of *Presence and Practice*.